Countervailing Powers

Riccardo Rosolino

Countervailing Powers

The Political Economy of Market, before and after Adam Smith

palgrave
macmillan

Riccardo Rosolino
Department of Human and Social Science
University of Naples—L'Orientale
Naples, Italy

ISBN 978-3-030-37801-1 ISBN 978-3-030-37802-8 (eBook)
https://doi.org/10.1007/978-3-030-37802-8

This Palgrave Macmillan imprint is published by the registered company Springer Nature Switzerland AG
The registered company address is: Gewerbestrasse 11, 6330 Cham, Switzerland

Acknowledgements

Writing a book is a somewhat solitary process. Nevertheless, a number of people have contributed to this process reaching its conclusion. Marco Fioravanti, Igor Mineo and Girolamo Imbruglia discussed the project with me from the early stages up to the final version. The suggestions of Rodolfo Savelli were decisive in identifying the documentary corpus that yielded the fil rouge of the book. I was also able to clarify several of the research hypotheses with Jean-Yves Grenier, who gave me valuable advice. In 2013, while I was a visiting scholar at Columbia University, I expounded my working theories at the seminars of the History Department, discussing them with Victoria de Grazia (who sponsored my New York visit), Charly Coleman, Martha Howell, Carl Wennerlind and Olindo De Napoli. Martha Howell and Carl Wennerlind generously dedicated some of their time to me, helping me to focus several points that were still unclear. I presented some of the results at the international conference *From Scotland to the South of the Mediterranean. The Thought of Adam Smith through Europe and Beyond* (Palermo, July 2017), where I was able to benefit from the valued criticism of Alberto Mingardi. Before the final draft of the book some of the results were published in two articles in 2017 and 2018: I am grateful to Iain Hampsher-Monk and the anonymous referees of *History of Political Thought* and to Marco Geuna and the anonymous referees of *Storia del pensiero politico* for having impelled me to clarify certain passages and elucidate some of the conclusions. After the publication of these first results I was offered valuable criticism by Maria Pia Paganelli. I should like to thank Laura Pacey first and then Ruth Noble at Palgrave Macmillan for having believed in my project. Lavanya Devgun was of great assistance in the preparation of the manuscript. Last but not least, with patience and professional skill Aelmuire Cleary revised and edited the text to ensure readability. Finally, although as I said at the beginning writing a book is always a solitary process, I have been lucky enough to share with Francesca de Tomasi both the less encouraging moments and the most exciting ones.

Contents

1 Introduction

The myth of the free-market persists unchallenged as one of the distinctive features of the Western world, despite the aura of failure attached to it since the latest crisis that exploded over ten years ago. In truth, the legend was merely grazed; nourished by undaunted faith it survives as one of the great utopias that, while unattainable, are nevertheless to be pursued. Beyond the setbacks, it continues to offer enticing glimpses of its feasibility. Yet, rarely, if ever, has this type of myth and the related worldview demonstrated such fragility as in the most recent economic downturn (Tooze 2018). For the stalwart champions of free-market efficiency it was disconcerting to have to acknowledge that market's incapacity to thwart attempts to manipulate the valuation processes of the goods exchanged. In the sense of a forum in which value is attributed to goods, the market proved incapable of both self-correction and self-regulation, eradicating—or at least undermining—the efficiency that was one of its chief strongpoints. At the same time, the crisis once again laid bare the congenital pathology afflicting the market—understood this time not merely as a forum but as an arena of opportunity in which individuals pursue their interests—namely, its exposure to the delinquent designs of those populating and driving it. These immoral strategies came up against no restrictions or sanctions of any kind. The very people who

R. Rosolino, *Countervailing Powers*,
https://doi.org/10.1007/978-3-030-37802-8_1

ought to have enforced the rules of the game, and who had every interest in doing so, were unable on their own to eliminate collusive behaviour aimed at whitewashing pernicious practices implemented in flagrant violation of the most elementary rules underpinning the logic of the market, first and foremost the principle of competition. There were definitely some who thought they could benefit from these highly speculative albeit not transparent activities,[1] but there were also many others who simply remained defenceless, watching the system crumble. Nonetheless, the liberal thinkers have always brandished the conviction that the market—with minimal support from the institutions guaranteeing judicial activity—would be able not only to monitor the performance of the game and the correct behaviour of the players but also, at the same time, to trigger the necessary mechanisms for sanctioning any foul play. Conversely, in the recent economic crisis two aspects came to the fore, both as frequently discussed as they are undervalued. Firstly, the functioning of the markets inevitably depends on necessary compliance with a series of rules, foremost among them the prohibition of backroom deals aimed at creating concentrations of power and the prohibition of strategies pursued through fraud and deception. Secondly, it has been clear since the very first records that markets have always been exposed to approaches tending to breach one or other of these rules, and often both.

As a result, one of the great lessons of Adam Smith's thought appears to be still able to tell us something. The self-sufficiency of the market is unconceivable without a supporting moral framework, for the simple reason that the alleged natural self-correcting and self-protecting mechanisms can be triggered only by the very people operating in the market (Barry 1990; Werhane 1991; Sen 2011; Sandmo 2016). Moreover, the relations of trust that these people benefit from and that fuel the market stem from agreement on and compliance with these same rules that the moral framework is built on.

However, this is only one side of the story. As I aim to show, it has long been thought (and still is by many people)[2] that the self-sufficiency of the

[1] This is, obviously, a constant in situations characterised by highly speculative activities. For a compelling historic picture I refer to Edward Chancellor (1999).

[2] Although it may seem paradoxical, this idea is anything but dead and buried, as I have demonstrated elsewhere (Rosolino 2013).

market, and the salvation of those who have fallen victim to conspiracies implemented through violence or fraud, could (and can) be achieved only by acknowledging the victims' right to resort to strategies of the same kind conducted using the same arms. This means that the market was conceived as capable of correcting and protecting itself, despite its structure as a place intrinsically bound to generate conflicts between subjects unwilling to adhere to the rationale of fair competition.[3] In actual fact, another intellectual approach preceded the liberal idea triggered by Smith's reflections, and later by classical political economy, and partially accompanied it almost as if it were a corollary. The path it followed appeared as discontinuous as it was—in the end—exceptionally consistent. The idea initially emerged in theological-moral circuits after which it was significantly employed in the world of law, which took over its essential core. It was then formidably applied in the thought of Smith, where it ended up assuming a distinctly political tone. Finally, the liberal thought of classical economics endowed it with the necessary elements to be remodelled in a strictly economic sense and adapted to the new scenarios of the modern age.

My research has been directed by two clues. Although these are apparently unconnected, without any tangible relation and distant in time, they immediately appeared to belong to the same sphere of investigation. The link that holds them together became the guiding thread of this book. They are two fragments: a couple of pages from one of the great classics of modern Western thought, Adam Smith's *An Inquiry into the Nature and Causes of the Wealth of Nations* (1776) and a fleeting passage

[3]This countervailing powers dynamic is different from that theorised by John K. Galbraith in the middle of the last century. In *American Capitalism* (1956), it was not only the monopolistic power of the unions that was accepted and recognised. Farmers' cooperatives were exempted from the antitrust measures, and retail chains were allowed to form large organisations in order to resist the market heft of the major manufacturers. According to Galbraith, this had two important results. In terms of commutative justice, the new entities engendered by the now pervasive logic of monopoly contributed to the establishment of a more equitable exchange dynamic. From the distributive perspective, the new balance of power allowed the actors engaging in exchanges to 'share out' the positive effects of a period of exceptional growth. In Galbraith's view, the principle of the balance of powers facilitated the autonomous self-regulation of the economy, reducing the need for government intervention to rein in the forces that otherwise tended to the formation of trusts.

in a legal text known only to specialists (but widely used in Europe during the seventeenth century until the first half of the eighteenth-century Europe), the *Tractatus de commerciis et cambio* (1619) by Sigismondo Scaccia.

In Book I, chapter viii (*On the Wages of Labour*) of his masterpiece Smith devotes a couple of pages to drawing attention to the fraudulent strategies of the capitalists, engaged in a sort of tacit agreement to elude the rationale of competition and keep wages low. It was the first time that someone had denounced the conspiracy that was underway, aimed at manipulating one of the principal novelties of industrial civilisation: the labour market. In putting his readers on their guard against what only those 'as ignorant of the world as of the subject' (Smith 1976, I.viii.13: 84) could be unaware of, Smith radically alters the interpretation hitherto provided of the wage-setting mechanism and hence of why wages remained at a level that could barely guarantee the workers' subsistence. It didn't take much to realise that it wasn't mere demographics that caused this effect; the inequitable relation of power between the conflicting interests was clearly undeniable (Stirati 1994: chs. 2–3). It derived from the fact that the workers were numerous, weak and disorganised and that the law forbade them to organise themselves, while the masters were few and hence found it easier to conspire and, above all, were protected by the state and evidently legitimised in acting in this way by social consensus. Smith believed that the crux of the problem lay in the conspiratorial monopolistic thrust that the masters could exert through tacit agreement. The practice of combinations—which is how Smith denoted the action of the masters—afflicted all markets, not just the new-born labour market. It was a species of disease, the most natural, possibly congenital, and definitely the most threatening and such agreements were the most eloquent illustration of it.

However, Smith does not settle for merely illustrating the problem. In his description of the way things were, alongside the word 'combination' there emerged another, 'resistance' (Rosolino 2018). Every so often the workers would resist, or attempt to resist, in ways that were often disordered and always illegal, since they were prohibited from organising themselves to define shared strategies. Ambiguously, Smith not only fails to suggest any way of getting out of this blind alley, but also leaves the two aspects of the issue—political and economic—vague and indistinct.

In addition to the right to resist a force that was in itself tyrannical, it was also possible to clearly discern the right to dispose freely of one's resources and negotiate the best price for one's labour, namely, the right to protection of one's contractual power. All this was trampled underfoot. Then there was the economic aspect related to the labour market, which was caught up in that stranglehold. Capitalism had put down its roots exploiting not so much the virtues of competition but the more formidable aspect of the fragility of the market.[4] Given that state intervention was almost always in the best case ineffective and in the worst case detrimental, there appeared to be no other choice. Without offering a clear answer, Smith left it to the reader to deduce the answers to the question. Was allowing the workers recourse to the same weapons as the capitalists the only way to restore room for manoeuvre to the wage-setting process and the natural trend of wages? Or, put another way, was allowing the opposing forces to counterbalance each other the only way to ensure that the competition mechanism could still mean something in the labour market? Chapter 2 of the book takes shape around this question and identifies the elements involved: no longer only moral and not yet entirely economic; no longer only legal and not yet entirely political.

Obviously, many people have dwelt on these pages of Smith, but they failed to realise that in these observations there was a—possibly unconscious—allusion to the idea of fighting fire with fire that was anything but new. They also failed to realise that this idea, in its original version and in Smith's formidable application of it, was part of an ideological trajectory fundamental for an understanding of how market self-sufficiency was conceived in the West.

The second clue guiding this investigation is found in a page of the *Tractatus de commerciis et cambio* by Sigismondo Scaccia, published in Rome in 1619, which states that resorting to one monopoly to thwart another does not constitute an offence. Conceived for the solution of a

[4]Fernand Braudel (1982: 230) spoke of 'the zone of the anti-market' to indicate where capitalism was positioned, 'today as in the past, before and after the industrial revolution'. Along the same lines, Pierre Bourdieu (2014: 94) makes observations that I find particularly pertinent: 'the regular order of the economic or burocratic cosmos is such that there is no struggle over the rules of the game. But there can be a struggle to change the rules of the game (by revolution or a policy of reform), which consist in cheating on the game and establishing a tacit regularity that will become the rule. Something that started off as cheating or casuistry or evasion…'.

case, this maxim had already been circulating in the theological world for over fifty years.[5] In adopting it, Scaccia not only legitimised it but also fostered its acquisition within another, one might say adjacent, discipline: the strictly juridical world of commercial law.[6] Why on earth would it be considered legitimate to resort to a monopoly to defend oneself against another monopoly? In the *Ancien Régime* culture, this particular term was used to indicate any action aimed at manipulating the dynamics of trade, and hence price-setting, using fraud or violence. More generally it was used to label any collusive agreement aimed at turning the operation of the marketplace to one's own advantage or at placing the other subjects involved—both as agents in the exchange and as competitors—in an inferior or disadvantaged position. Finally, irrespective of exactly what the deplorable conduct in question was, almost everywhere in Europe and for a good part of the modern age, the monopoly was considered both a crime and a sin. Anyone who gave in to the *tyrannical vice*—one of the epithets frequently used to describe it—was nothing less than a cheat and a traitor, since his position of strength was the result not only of having cheated others but also of having betrayed the ethical and moral code that was even then considered instrumental to the functioning of the market. Every monopoly, in whatever of its myriad forms, was a swindle and every monopolist—never considered singly but always in cahoots with others—was a traitor. Moreover, in the shady attempt to acquire a preferential position of strength or superiority with a view to controlling the dynamics of trade, the monopolist—or more often the clique of monopolists—naturally became a dangerous creature for the entire community and ultimately for the state. So, why on earth permit recourse to this same behaviour, albeit as an exceptional measure, as a form of resistance? How on earth did so many theologians (primarily Dominicans and Jesuits) permit the entrenchment of a juridical and moral principle such as *monopolium vs. monopolium* that was both heterodox and a potential harbinger of war and destruction? Chapter 3 of the book traces the process through which this principle was generated,

---

[5]The first record of the maxim is to be found in Domingo de Soto (1582).

[6]Scaccia's statement was noted by Roman Piotrowski (1933: 206–207), who nevertheless failed to discern its scope or understand what lay beneath it and hence deemed it marginal.

the various scenarios in which it was applied and the issues of a moral character stemming from it. It also explores how this principle was appropriated in the field of commercial law and the questions it brought with it. Although all this took place between the sixteenth and seventeenth centuries, and hence a long time before Smith, it nevertheless seems possible to glimpse in the background the conviction that the market was indeed equipped with the means to neutralise its congenital frailty and that it was the very actors in the market who could express and implement this means. However, at the same time it also seems as though we can see something contradictory or paradoxical. The congenital weakness affecting the market, and that these same actors had to rid it of, was none other than the effect of their relentless and uncontrollable inclination to stack the deck and to line up as monopolists in front of each other in the garb of sellers or buyers.

In any case, in the theological and juridical arguments it was precisely the rupture of social harmony engendered by the potentially tyrannical presence of the monopolist that legitimised recourse to the same rationale. In this way, the idea behind allowing fire to be fought with fire was to achieve the natural restoration of order and the salvation of the community. Meanwhile, however, the appropriation of the right of resistance revealed the political character of a market conceived as a battlefield, the functioning of which was not limited to the dynamic of competition.[7] Anyone falling victim to the violence of a group of players guilty of rigging the game through a monopolistic conspiracy was entitled to act likewise.

The principle of *monopolium vs. monopolium*, which inspired a notion of the market that was anything but peaceful, enjoyed a vast circulation in the world of theology whence it migrated to the strictly juridical realm. But in the final decades of the seventeenth century it began to fade to the point of disappearing from sight. It had, moreover, always been a principle triggered by heterodox convictions. Chapter 4 pivots on this disappearance—a clue in itself—which turned out to be temporary, a

[7] For a twentieth-century reading of the market in these terms, see the classic work by Max Weber (1978: 93).

species of eclipse, one of the signs of the discontinuity mentioned at the beginning.

When the physiocrats reconceived the market as a place where there is nothing to be gained from resorting to fraud, lies and delinquent strategies and where the various interests will naturally find a harmonious order, the principle of *monopolium vs. monopolium* was rendered meaningless. The new theory held that the elimination of players fraudulently aspiring to positions of strength would take place without any great friction or trouble. When, in these same decades, Smith showed himself at pains to demonstrate that the operation of the market was riddled with conflict which was generated by the market itself and very hard to root out, he was once again going against the flow.

In truth, although the old notion which held that fire was the best antidote for fire had been eclipsed it had not been entirely forgotten. Or rather it was, paradoxically, precisely by virtue of this idea that it was possible to leave the state more on the sidelines than the physiocrats had thought to do, in the conviction that the market would be saved not so much as a result of the effects of its at once virtuous and abstract rationale, but rather as a result of the actions of resistance implemented against those who violated its rules and dynamics.

But Smith was not alone in realising how much the markets were threatened by delinquent strategies, he was not alone in observing the looming threat of the monopolising principle, and nor was he alone in seeing that all forms of social aggregation around specific interests represented a potential weapon for sabotage of the competition mechanism and subversion of social order. However, no one was to remember the importance he gave to the word 'resistance' in the conflict-of-interest dynamics that the new capitalist culture had put on the agenda. Some elements of his thought were forgotten and others completely distorted (Rothschild 2001: ch. 2). In focusing on the second phase of rupture and silence involving the ideological trajectory in question, Chapter 5 will explore how Smith's thought was exploited and manipulated in the decade preceding the emanation of the *Combination Acts* (1799–1800) and in the two decades following, through to their abolition in 1824–1825.

When the principle of *monopolium vs. monopolium* reappeared in the full flush of the liberal ferment in support of the notion of a self-sufficient market, it did so cloaked in one of the great convictions of classical economics. Any social aggregation, however powerful or threatening, had to be free to pursue its strategies in support of its interests. This freedom would ensure that no such aggregation could act in isolation and the power of each of them would perforce find its natural counterweight. Paradoxical as it might seem, it was the market itself and the competition at its core that demanded this.

It took fifty years before Smith's words were reconsidered in the conviction that both capitalists and workers had to be left free to combine or agree to define shared strategies to pursue their interests. At this point the old principle had become definitively legitimised, although possibly unrecognisable. Smith's concerns appeared insubstantial and, by now, obsolete. In the eyes of John Ramsey McCulloch, and of his teacher David Ricardo, to disarm monopolistic conspiracies and neutralise the gigantic presences they generated, it was sufficient to allow them to tackle each other freely. What had for centuries been considered most threatening and deleterious was nothing more or less than the life force of society. Once they were rendered free, recourse to practices that had always been considered conspiracies would in the long run become gradually and silently weaker and fainter. This entirely predictable disappearance was by now in the way of things; in a natural and spontaneous manner the now unshackled 'giants' would prove innocuous before the big numbers of economics. Precisely because of these numbers, it was practically impossible and decidedly unrealistic to imagine manipulating the competition mechanism.

References

Barry, N. 1990. Adam Smith and the Ethics of Capitalism. In *Adam Smith's Legacy. His Thought in Our Time*, ed. N. Elliott, 92–100. London: Adam Smith Institute.

Bourdieu, P. 2014 [2012]. *On the State. Lectures at the Collège de France, 1989–1992*, ed. P. Champagne, R. Lenoir, F. Poupeau, and M.-C. Rivière. Cambridge: Polity.

Braudel, F. 1982 [1979]. *Civilization and Capitalism, 15th–18th Century*, Vol. II: *The Wheels of Commerce*. London: William Collins Sons & Co.

Chancellor, E. 1999. *Devil Take the Hindmost. A History of Financial Speculation*. London: Macmillan.

Galbraith, J.K. 1956 [1952]. *American Capitalism. The Concept of Countervailing Power*. Harmondsworth: Penguin.

Piotrowski, R. 1933. *Cartels and Trusts. Their Origin and Historical Development from the Economic and Legal Aspects*. London: Allen & Unwin.

Rosolino, R. 2013. Vices tyranniques. Résistance au monopole, idéologie et marché à l'aube de la modernité. *Annales HSS* 68 (3): 793–819.

Rosolino, R. 2018. Resisting Economic Conspiracies: Adam Smith, the (Labour) Market, and the Moral Basis of Antimonopolistic Resistance. *History of Political Thought* 39 (2): 297–324.

Rothschild, E. 2001. *Economic Sentiments. Adam Smith, Condorcet and the Enlightenment*. London and Cambridge, MA: Harvard University Press.

Sandmo, A. 2016. Adam Smith and Modern Economics. In *Adam Smith: His Life, Thought, and Legacy*, ed. R.P. Hanley, 231–246. Princeton, NJ and Oxford: Princeton University Press.

Scaccia, S. 1619. *Tractatus de commerciis et cambio*. Romae: Brugiotti.

Sen, A. 2011. Uses and Abuses of Adam Smith. *History of Political Economy* 43 (2): 257–271.

Smith, A. 1976 [1776]. *An Inquiry into the Nature and Causes of the Wealth of Nations*, 2 vols., ed. R.H. Campbell and A.S. Skinner. Oxford: Oxford University Press.

Soto (de), D. 1582 [1553]. *De iustitia et iure*. Lugduni: Honorato.

Stirati, A. 1994. *The Theory of Wages in Classical Economics. A Study of Adam Smith, David Ricardo and Their Contemporaries*. Aldershot and Brookfield: Edward Elgar.

Tooze, A. 2018. *Crashed. How a Decade of Financial Crises Changed the World*. New York: Viking.

Weber, M. 1978 [1922]. *Economy and Society*, ed. G. Roth and C. Wittich. Berkeley, Los Angeles, and London: University of California Press.

Werhane, P.H. 1991. *Adam Smith and His Legacy for Modern Capitalism*. Oxford: Oxford University Press.

2

Adam Smith, Workers' Rights and the Political Side of the Market

Capitalists Stack the Deck

There's something seductive about the script that casts capitalism as the last to arrive on the scene, making its appearance only when everything is ready and waiting. Capitalism did not have to invent the market, still less production and consumption. It did not even have to create hierarchies; it just made use of what was at hand. Then, obviously, it distorted all of the above, bending them to its purposes (Braudel 1977: 75). We might add that as soon as the dust had settled (perhaps before, even), it took the precaution of rewriting the rules of the game, rendering ephemeral what would become—not without a degree of bad faith—one of the great illusions of capitalist culture: the rationale of competition, the soul of the self-regulating market. Paradoxically, Adam Smith himself was one of the first to expose the whole process, to show how capitalism had put down roots by manipulating the competition mechanism in one of the key sectors of the new industrial civilisation, that is, in the sphere of labour. It's frequently said that Smith was not fully cognisant of the profound

R. Rosolino, *Countervailing Powers*,
https://doi.org/10.1007/978-3-030-37802-8_2

changes taking place in the world that he was observing. Clearly, this was one element that did not escape him.

Smith shared with both his friend David Hume and many of the physiocrats the conviction that wages would perforce settle at the minimum subsistence level. Hume emphasised how the poor conditions of workers made it difficult for them to agree together an effective common strategy.[1] And Necker was of the same opinion. Employers would pay as little for labour as possible since they could choose the workers who offered themselves most cheaply. The outcome of the bargaining process was thus distorted. For Turgot, too, it was obvious that the workers, who were numerous, had no other resource than their labour, whereas employers were still few and free of any compulsion to pay a premium for manpower. As a result of this fierce competition for jobs (unlike in America, where there was a shortage of workmen) wages were constantly forced downwards (Turgot 2011a: 8). Necker added that workers' circumstances were further compromised by the effects of social legislation that reinforced the existing dynamic, although he drew attention to the small group of countries where 'that form of slavery' was tempered by political rights which afforded a small 'margin of resistance'. In England, such rights were most evidently guaranteed due to the nature of its government. In both *Sur la législation et le commerce des grains* (1775) and *De l'administration des finances de la France* (1784), Necker used the word *résistance* when referring to these rights.[2]

[1]'Where the labourers and artisans are accustomed to work for low wages, and to retain but a small part of the fruits of their labour, it is difficult for them, even in a free government, to better their condition, or conspire among themselves to heighten their wages. But even where they are accustomed to a more plentiful way of life, it is easy for the rich, in an arbitrary government, to conspire against them, and throw the whole burthen of the taxes on their shoulders' (Hume 1752: 16).

[2]'L'Angleterre est le pays du monde où la condition du peuple paroît la meilleure; cette heureuse circonstance ne peut pas être attribuée à la modération de impôts, puisque, proportion gardée, ils sont plus considérable que dans aucun autre pays de l'Europe; il faut plutôt en chercher le cause dans la nature du gouvernement, qui donne au peuple un degré de force et de *résistance* qui influe sur le prix de ses salaires' (italics mine) (Necker 1820a: I, 313). 'La classe de la société, dont le sort se trouve comme fixé par l'effet des loix sociales, est composée de tous ceux qui vivant du travail de leurs mains, reçoivent impérieusement la loi des propriétaires, et sont forcés de se contenter du salaire proportionné aux simples nécessités de la vie: leur concurrence et l'urgence de leurs besoins, constituent leur état de dépendance; et ces circonstances ne peuvent point changer. Tous les temps, tous les pays, présentent le même spectacle, et il n'y a d'exception,

Smith's position on the issue was entirely original. It was not only a question of numbers. It was certainly true that workers were numerous and capitalists few, but the reason that wages stayed at subsistence level was due to the fact that, instead of competing between themselves, the employers were tacitly involved in an agreement to fix the bargaining process:

> The masters being fewer in number, can combine much more easily; and the law, besides, authorises, or at least does not prohibit their combinations, while it prohibits those of the workmen. We have no acts of parliament against combining to lower the price of work; but many against combining to raise it. In all such disputes the masters can hold out much longer. A landlord, a farmer, a master manufacturer, or merchant, though they did not employ a single workman, could generally live a year or two upon the stocks which they have already acquired. Many workmen could not subsist a week, few could subsist a month, and scarce any a year without employment. In the long-run the workman may be as necessary to his master as his master is to him; but the necessity is not so immediate. (Smith 1976, I.viii.12: 83–84)

The word Smith uses to describe the conspiratorial process, 'combination',[3] was applied only to the workers' side of the equation in the legislation of the day—a series of restrictive measures enacted throughout the eighteenth century (Orth 1987: 181–190).[4] For some decades,

il n'y a d'adoucissement, à cette espece d'esclavage, que dans le petit nombre d'états, où la forme du gouvernement, laisse entre les mains du peuple quelque droit politique, dont la jouissance influe sur la considération, et lui procure quelque moyen de *résistance*' (italics mine) (Necker 1820b: V, 323).

[3]As noted, by way of example, by James Moher (1988: 92), 'The Combination Laws were a product of a highly regulated medieval society. Originally they were aimed at suppressing associations of both masters and journeymen—traders as well as producers—to prevent them raising the prices of their products and services. Apart from being regarded by the courts as a restraint of trade, such combinations were viewed by the legislature as conspiracies and as tending to usurp the wage-setting functions of the State'.

[4]The tailors' strike of 1720 provided the occasion for the passing of the first Combination Act as well as for an early prosecution of workmen for criminal conspiracy; the act voided all contracts, covenants or agreements for raising wages or reducing hours. Six years later, in 1726, new legislation covered the venerable wool trade, and in the middle of the century 'the statutory ban on combination was expanded to include trades other than tailoring and weaving' (Orth

it had been the workers who had been accused of resorting to conspiracies of every sort aimed to keep their remuneration at the highest possible level and, more generally, to improve their conditions of work (Malcomson 1984).[5] Smith turned that scenario—by now part of a popular mindset—on its head. In fact, he went further: he showed how numbers contributed to disguise the real state of affairs which, if looked at more attentively, was actually quite different.

> We rarely hear, it has been said, of the combinations of masters; though frequently of those of workmen. But whoever imagines, upon this account, that masters rarely combine, is as ignorant of the world as of the subject. Masters are always and everywhere in a sort of tacit, but constant and uniform combination, not to raise the wages of labour above their actual rate. To violate this combination is every where a most unpopular action, and a sort of reproach to a master among his neighbours and equals. We seldom, indeed, hear of this combination, because it is the usual, and one may say, the natural state of things which nobody ever hears of. Masters too sometimes enter into particular combinations to sink the wages of labour even below this rate. These are always conducted with the utmost silence and secrecy, till the moment of execution, and when the workmen yield, as they sometimes do, without resistance, though severely felt by them, they are never heard of by other people. Such combinations, however, are frequently resisted by a contrary defensive combination of the workmen, who sometimes too, without any provocation of this kind, combine of their own accord to raise the price of their labour. (Smith 1976, I.viii.13: 84)

Wage levels were not only the result of the conspiratorial behaviour of masters, who were much better placed than workers to pursue their own

---

1987: 189). For the next fifty years, legislation against combination continued for particular trades until the general Combination Act of 1799 (Orth 1991: 5–24).

[5]As demonstrated by Robert W. Malcomson (1984), workers' actions had reached a certain organisational level. 'For while many combined actions were certainly conservative in character—they involved an appeal to the law, and dutiful petitions to the local magistrates; they revealed a respect for patriarchal authority—other combinations were much more self-assertive and much less differential. In certain places and in certain circumstances workers claimed for themselves an independent authority: they made "unauthorised" claims to control some of their own conditions of labour, and to obtain justice for themselves; they claimed the right to act in their own interest' (Malcomson 1984: 157).

interests. They were also related to the fact that the workers were unable to appeal to the judicial system (since there was no legislation for their protection) or employ any measures to defend themselves against attack.

Smith may have been the first to openly denounce the conspiracy in which the capitalists were tacitly involved, but it should have already been obvious enough, even common knowledge. Only an ignoramus—as Smith himself said—could claim to know nothing about it. And those who did, kept dishonestly silent. Smith actually did much more than demonstrate how common assumptions had helped to misrepresent the reality of the clash between employers and workers and to justify existing legislation. He began by informing his readers what lay behind this conflict of interests and went on to suggest, without much in the way of clarification, how the trap into which the wage-setting process had fallen (or been made to fall) might be deactivated. Although they did react from time to time, workers possessed no effective means of *resisting* and thwarting the conspiratorial manoeuvres against them. Their rebellions were usually rowdy and unpopular, typically characterised by recklessness and desperation. They were almost always violent, and in any case illegal. By law, each individual was supposed to act alone, with such contractual leverage as he (or she) might have with respect to an employer. When it happened otherwise, when the workers had been galvanised by the idea of making their case collectively, in however fragmented and disorganised a fashion, the forces of law were ever ready to intervene at the request and on the side of the capitalists. Conversely, agreements between the latter were never subjected to regulation. The state chose simply not to see what could have been difficult—if not impossible—to prove, let alone punish. The agreements (combinations) to which Smith referred were not the outcome of actual negotiation, still less of formally signed contracts. Nonetheless, the fact that they were implicit did not necessarily make them fragile. Anyone stepping out of line—Smith notes—would find himself the target of vilification by the tacit co-conspirators and by others as well. Despite not being signed and sealed, the bond of solidarity made itself felt, not least through the knowledge that its violation would provoke the hostility of a master's 'neighbours and equals'. Smith was suggesting that harmony between employers would rapidly morph into a less benign moral pressure if the conspiratorial project was jeopardised by the rash behaviour of a renegade (Stirati 1994: 59–60). Breaking the tacit agreement was neither convenient nor socially expedient. If human actions were spurred by interest, on the one hand, and by the desire for social approval, on the other hand, adherence to the conspiracy allowed entrepreneurs to both favour their own advantage and to acquire the consensus of others.

Furthermore—as Necker had observed—the form that the conflict had settled into was also legitimised by the common perception of things, or what Necker called the 'social laws' (Necker 1820b: 323). The formal legislation that had persisted over decades had come to be seen as tradition, although already the industrial revolution was undermining many of that tradition's certainties. Finally, there were the very latest economic and political theories. James Steuart had recently homed in on the deleterious effects of solidarity agreements between workers on the costs of production and the national trade balance. He argued that this called for state intervention to correct such distortions of the market, which contaminated the world of work and must therefore be actively discouraged. At the same time, it would be beneficial to encourage competition between job seekers so that wages would settle at near subsistence level, or as Steuart called it: *the physically necessary* (Steuart 1767: I, 311–319).[6]

In many respects, Smith's position was thoroughly heterodox. As he argued, workers who had no disposable income were effectively denied access to the markets as consumers, which had a negative effect on the nation's enrichment. He also made it abundantly clear that he thought the unequal treatment of masters and men was profoundly iniquitous, contrary to any 'system of natural liberty', and an abuse of natural rights. Without specifically proposing it as a solution, Smith put the thorny question to his readers: should not the workers too be allowed to form

[6]On the relevance of Steuart's passages, I refer to Samuel Hollander (1973: 44). Some considerations not far from Steuart's reasoning had been made by Josiah Tucker: 'Foreigners can never get rich in a strange Country, but by working cheaper or better than the Natives. And if they do so, though Individuals may suffer, the Publick is certainly a Gainer; as there is so much Merchandize to be exported upon cheaper Terms, or so much saved to the Merchant, whereby he may afford to export the cheaper. Not to mention, That by this means the Price of Labour is continually beat down, Combinations of Journeymen against their Masters are prevented, Industry is encouraged, and an Emulation exicited' (Tucker 1750: 42). On this passage as an element indicative of the importance that the collective actions of the workers had taken in determining 'income distribution', I refer to Stirati (1994: 19–20).

agreements to defend themselves against the (more or less tacit and clandestine) conspiratorial tactics of employers? It was indeed an old question and had arrived in modern times through a circuitous and surprising route. Its link to the past lay in the fact that Smith—as we will see in the next chapter—was merely redeploying an old idea that held it to be morally justified to resist a monopolistic conspiracy (and the combinations were nothing if not that) by using the same weapons as the conspirators. The idea first made its appearance in theological circles in the mid-sixteenth century and was then taken up and completely reworked by the world of commercial law in the seventeenth century. It has persisted up to our own times, being taken up in Smith's reformulated terms by the new classical political economy of the 1820s to legitimise the unionisation of the workforce and regulate the economic aspect of the class conflict (as we shall see in Chapter 5).[7] In this fashion it was to become, in the first instance, the theoretical basis and justification for the expediency of collective bargaining and, subsequently, a demonstration in economic and political terms of the essential inoffensiveness of a capitalism of powerful vested interests. The latter, for all their potency, were nonetheless limited because 'natural' opponents would be armed with the same monopolistic weapons.[8] Though still giants, the powerful would no longer have the power to instil fear.

Vulnerable Interests

The ambiguity that (not untypically) bedevils Smith's two pages on this issue meant that, in the 1790s, his words were recruited both to support measures under which combinations (of workers and capitalists alike) were outlawed, and also to oppose them. Indeed, Smith would be cited again in 1824–1825—as he was in 1799–1800—in support of the abolition of the very measures approved a quarter of a century earlier.[9]

[7] See Geoffrey Ingham (2008: ch. V).

[8] We find the explicit theorising of this in John K. Galbraith (1956).

[9] On the misuse of Smith's ideas, see Emma Rothschild (2001: ch. 2) and Amartya Sen (2011). We will return to this topic in the Chapter 5.

His deliberations do, in effect, range over a number of questions. Historians of economics and political thought have written about Smith's sympathy for the poor, his concern for a fragile emergent working class (Phelps Brown 1976: 246–252), his distrust of the industrial class (Pack 1991: 140–160; Elliott 2000: 449) and, finally, his not-quite-so-liberal way of looking at the new power relationships spawned by capitalism (McNulty 1973: 353–363; Elliott 2000; Pack 1991; Perelman 2000: 194–195; Evensky 2005a: 123; Ron 2008: 128–129). Smith's words are even more surprising because they do not align with the beliefs he expounded elsewhere in the same work, specifically with regard to the sphere of state intervention, the efficiency of a market based on fair play and the role of justice in the construction of a moral order (Young 2005). Smith's considerations are not congruent with the belief that the state should intervene to punish unjust conduct, particularly commercial practices that do not comply with the rules of fair play. As we know, Smith explicitly recognised three areas of government activity as consistent with his conception of system of natural liberty (Smith 1976, IV.ix.51: 687–688); and, as has been pointed out, 'the most significant task which governments are required to undertake is the establishment of a legal framework, without which no market can function' (Hamowy 1987: 20–21).[10]

At the same time, the remarkably optimistic notion of an economic scenario shaped by a competitive game of interests conducted with a proper respect for the rules, in which those interests would emerge harmonised due to the inherent virtues of the market, clearly conflicted with a more pessimistic vision in which interests remain in conflict and the game is conducted in the most inequitable manner imaginable through the expedient of combination (Alvey 2003: 190–192; Turpin 2011: 40, 43–45; Herzog 2013a: chs. 4–6; Herzog 2013b).[11]

---

[10] See Cohen (1989: 69–70). This aspect, widely discussed by Smith's readers, has recently been revisited by Evensky (2005b: 111–113) and Sandmo (2016: 239), who observes that 'an important role for government was to design an economic system that as far as possible discouraged the creation of private cartels and monopolies'. See also Hill (2016: 34–41).

[11] According to Force (2003: 86) labelling Smith's attitude using 'the terms "optimistic" and "pessimistic" may in fact be misleading'.

Adam Smith's views on issues such as wage levels and the relations between employers and workers set him at quite a distance from the ideas of the physiocrats, despite the fact that he was on friendly terms with many of them. Among these, Le Mercier de la Rivière was perhaps the one who had most clearly expressed the idea of a world in which everyone's interests were mutually dependent as a result of reciprocal fulfilment and could hence be seen as harmonised within a single system (Le Mercier de la Rivière 1767).[12] Furthermore, not only could interests interact in a far from harmonious manner (Schumpeter 2006: 225; Brubaker 2006: 182), but the manifestly immoral conspiratorial strategies with which such interests were too often pursued were, at best, difficult to condemn and, at worst, impossible to control. Lastly, Smith had drawn attention in no uncertain terms to two inextricably linked factors: firstly, behind an apparent reality lurked a grave injustice, that different weights and measures were applied to masters and workers; secondly, if state intervention were neither conceivable or desirable, the only remaining possibility was to allow such conspiratorial strategies to be countered by resistance action of the same immoral kind. In assuming this position, Smith abandoned the idea of possible judiciary action against those who did not abide by the logic of free and fair competition. Albeit ambiguously, was he paving the way for a new approach in which the market and its moral/legal order would not need to be protected from one of its most feared threats: the monopolistic rationale of conspiratorial agreements?

Without saying it in so many words, Smith seems willing to accept recourse to resistance as the only way for workers to avoid being crushed by the perpetual aggression and tacit conspiracy of capitalists. In the face of such an assault, it would appear that the only defence possible is the use of equivalent weapons. This specifically reflects his open attitude and indulgence towards the possibility of workers' resistance, which should be reconsidered from a legal and moral standpoint. Without explicitly

[12]It was an order 'ou tous le intérêts sont si perfaitement combinés, si inséparablement unis entre eux, que depuis les Souverains jusq'au dernier de eurs sujets, le bonheur des uns ne peut s'accroître que par le bonheur des autres' (Le Mercier de la Rivière 1767: *Discourse préliminaire*, VII). On this topic, I refer to Sheehan and Wahrman (2015: chs. 6–7).

approving the idea (Kennedy 2008: 146),[13] Smith pointed the way to doing so, as indeed happened some decades later. Equally implicitly, he had exposed the less edifying—strictly 'political' and conflictual—side of the market. What is surprising, though, is that what must have seemed a pessimistic prospect in Smith's eyes would be presented as a motive for optimism by the new classical political economy of liberal stamp. Society had shown a capacity for organising itself through its own efforts, and the market had proven capable of curing itself, without any outside interference, of its congenital and most dangerous pathology.

Therefore, Smith's implicit indulgent attitude towards a possible moral (and political) legitimisation of workers' actions embraced two lines of philosophical and/or moral reasoning, tending on the one hand towards the juridical, with regard to the right of self-defence, and on the other towards the purely political, with respect to the right to resist.

To resist was a natural human right.[14] In his *Lectures on Jurisprudence*, Smith said as much specifically, placing the issue in a strictly political and constitutional context and invoking Locke.[15] He went on to examine legitimate defence of the person and property, citing his mentor Hutcheson.[16] He used the term 'resistance' again in the *Wealth of Nations*, in a purely political sense, referencing historical events in which communities, cities or kingdoms had had to defend themselves.

---

[13]Nevertheless, 'there is no suggestion, explicit or implicit, that combinations of workers should be permitted. As a moral philosopher educated in the school of Natural Law, he favoured perfect liberty, pure and simple, and followed his analysis wherever it took him without fear or favour to any special interests group. He favoured neither side in the determination of wages, but was not blind to the unfair consequences of the existing arrangements' (Kennedy 2008: 146).

[14]For Smith, natural rights 'fall into two categories according to the injuries which can be done to an individual in his person and in his reputation. The former are subdivided into injuries to life and body, and injury to a person's liberty to move around and combine with other people in marriage, business, etc. These are undoubtedly the most obvious rights of all' (Haakonssen 1981: 103).

[15]Smith 1978, Report of 1762–3, v.68: 297; v.112–115: 315–316; v.131–134: 322–323; Report dated 1766, 82: 429; 93–95: 434–435. In the debate on the right of resistance Smith's position was certainly known, and tended to be assimilated to the conservative views of David Hume, William Blackstone and Edmund Burke (Dickinson 1994: 171).

[16]Smith 1978, Report of 1762–3, ii.107: 111; ii.115–116: 114–115; ii.147: 127.

To what category should the actions of workers labelled as defence or resistance be ascribed? If to resist was a natural right, and if it has always been thought important to emphasise the relevance of the natural rights tradition in Smith's thought (Stein 1979; Haakonssen 1981; Clark 1988; Young 2008), is it not equally important to analyse the particular passage where he sets about describing the conflict of interest between workers and employers and weighs the juridical and moral aspects of workers' self-defence and resistance? Smith never uses the latter word (or others deriving from the same root) in a loose or generic manner. He employs 'resistance' on another ten occasions in the *Wealth of Nations*, always with a clearly political meaning,[17] not in a constitutional sense, but in the wider and more ambiguous schema of friend/enemy, as later theorised by Carl Schmitt (1976).

To avoid misunderstanding, I should clarify that it is not my intention to propose yet another divergent reading of Smith's thought in this sphere. As has rightly been noted, 'Smith's politics often seem inconsistent and even contradictory. One example of this is his apparently conflicted attitude to capitalism and the free market, which has baffled some scholars and even given rise to suggestions that he is proto-Marxist' (Hill 2016: 322).[18] In fact, Smith's words do not anticipate anything very revolutionary. The conflictual dimension is described and interpreted in what we might call a 'conservative' framework. The workers' actions—assuming that in his eyes they have an intrinsic moral and/or political legitimacy—are meant to defend liberties and rights that have been trampled on, to preserve or restore an order that has been violated and to revitalise a compromised *modus operandi* (competition). Admittedly, Smith expresses (vague) apprehension about the need to counteract a situation arising from fraud perpetrated against workers and, more generally, against the principles of the free market. If the market is founded on competition and that competition presupposes certain rules, chiefly that covert deals falsifying the dynamics of the game (with an outcome

[17]Smith 1976, III.iii.8: 401–402; IV.iii.c.71: 620; V.i.a.5: 692; V.i.a.35: 703; V.i.a.36: 704–705; V.i.a.37: 705; V.i.a: 708; V.i.e.28: 753; V.i.g.22: 802; V.i.g.30: 806.

[18]Those that seem contradictions for Lisa Hill are instead, for Sergio Cremaschi (1989), moral tensions inside Adam Smith's thinking.

that would be a foregone conclusion) are inadmissible, then the conspiratorial strategy behind combinations is a betrayal of the market's very logic. Besides, this creates the preconditions for a double injustice. As a consequence of tacit agreements between masters, workers cannot hope to negotiate a just recompense for their labour; nor do they have recourse to any legitimate form of defence or resistance, since under existing legislation they are denied any sort of collective action.

Yet the rights to defend oneself and to resist have their own juridical and moral, not to say political, validity. We should not forget that for Smith, the basis for rights is injury (Haakonssen 2016: 54)[19] and that in defence of his life, the integrity of his person, his possessions and his family, every man had the right to use the same level of violence used against him. Just as in the event of tyrannical behaviour, it was politically legitimate to resist, and even to take up arms against the constituted authority guilty of abuse or threatening to be so. In both cases, it was legitimate to repel force with force, and in the case in question here, for the defensive or resistant action of workers to be effective, they would have to avail themselves of the same weapons as those deployed by the capitalists.

As we know, Smith's understanding of the concept of self-defence and the right to resist (Smith 1978, Report of 1762–3, v.128–140: 321–326)[20] derived from his reading Grotius and Locke, as well as the teachings of his tutor Francis Hutcheson, who had, in turn, borrowed many ideas from his own teacher, Gershom Carmichael. Unlike Samuel Pufendorf[21]—who had imagined that 'the cultivation and preservation of sociable living obliged all members of society to obey superior powers', namely husbands, fathers, masters and rulers—Carmichael maintained

[19]'In recognizing something as injury to a person, we ascribe that in which the person has been injured as a right to the injured person—his or her physical integrity, freedom of movement, property in things, voluntary relations with other individuals, and so on' (Haakonssen 2016: 54).

[20]He devoted an entire lesson of his course on *Jurisprudence* to the right of resistance, which was examined in a purely historical and constitutional context (Haakonssen 1981: 127–132).

[21]Another writer who had represented an important benchmark in Smith's intellectual development in relation to natural law; in fact he is immediately cited (Smith 1978, Report of 1762–3, i.1215: 8–9. I refer to Taylor (1965: 3–28, 63–72), Haakonssen (1981), Teichgraeber (1986: 68), and to Phillipson (2010: chs. 3–6).

that 'every individual ha[d] a natural right of self-defence' and 'a right to property in things on which he has laboured'; and he insisted that the right of resistance was nothing but 'a corollary of the respect for oneself and for others required by the law of nature' (Moore and Silverthorne 2002: XII–XIII).

Many of the theories that shaped Smith's beliefs derived from Hutcheson's ideas. These included the right to resist, which is as weak and helpless in Pufendorf's view as it is vigorous and radical in Carmichael's. Hutcheson's theory of rights was based on exactly the same assumption used to define men's inherent sociability prior to law and government. It also 'included a defense of a right of resistance that Pufendorf had specifically excluded' (Teichgraeber 1986: 68). Hutcheson insisted that all rights must be divided into perfect and imperfect categories 'according as they are more or less necessary to the preservation of a social life' (Hutcheson 1747: 112).[22] The violation of perfect rights (our right to life, to the fruits of our labour, and to faithful performance of contracts) makes life intolerable.[23] These rights have a predominantly economic character; and 'since by definition violation of perfect rights made life intolerable', it is possible to use 'violence to secure such rights when threatened' (Teichgraeber 1986: 51). Hutcheson hinted that the exercise of the right of resistance—in extreme cases—could even be conceived beyond its strictly constitutional scope: 'The perfidy of a superior may set his subjects free from all obligation to him: and even a slave may have a right of violently resisting a savage and barbarous master, tho' he had been subjected to slavery for the justest reasons' (Hutcheson 1755: II, 272).

[22]'Perfect rights are of such necessity that a general allowing them to be violated must entirely destroy all society: and therefor such rights ought to be maintained to all even by violence: and severest punishments inflicted upon the violation of them' (Hutcheson 1747: 112).

[23]As has been pointed out by Haakonssen (1996: 81–82), 'Mankind being what it is, this will on the whole mean that the negatively defined rights—rights not to be injured—or perfect rights, have practical priority over the positively defined rights—rights to receive some good—or imperfect rights'. See also Stein (1979: 626–634).

That said, he is clearly aware of the weight of power asymmetries and of the fact that 'the labourers are compelled to make employment contracts because they have only their labour to sell and have no control of the means of production'; nevertheless, he describes 'the relationship in terms of mutual cooperation maintained on the basis of their legal equality in spite of their economic inequality' (Ogose 2003: 50).

Smith went several steps beyond his master's reasoning, not least because the objective reality he was examining was notably different from that of twenty years earlier. If, as Hutcheson had argued, wage levels ought to reflect the value of the corresponding labour rendered, the problem was to establish a reasonable exchange rate. Hutcheson also noted how, in recent times, the dependency relationship between masters and workers had been affected by increases in population and employment and by the enclosure of land (Hutcheson 1755: II, 199).[24] But Smith was looking elsewhere, taking note of something that had been concealed behind a veil of ignorance and deceit: tacit conspiracies had taken root in the fledgling industrial society, embittering the conflict between capitalists and workers and making the latter's conditions less bearable. These were the most dangerous threats to the supposed harmony that the new *laissez faire* regime should have guaranteed.

[24]'As soon as mankind were considerably increased in numbers, and the more fertile clear lands occupied, many accidents would occasion that a great many would have no property, nor any opportunity of employing their labours on goods of their own for their support: and many on the other hand who had much property would need the labours of others, be willing to support them on this account, and give them further compensation: this would introduce the relation of master and servant' (Hutcheson 1755: II, 199).

Must Wages Be Low?

We know that Smith considered it right as well as advantageous for wages to be as high as possible.[25] Having said that, he did not think the condition of the workers unjust per se. If the market—as a 'natural problem solver' (Herzog 2013a: 11 and ch. 3)—were allowed to function properly, the distribution of resources would be more equitable, or in any case different from what capitalism in its infancy was bringing about (Hill 2020: ch. 3). He certainly saw it as imperative to create the preconditions for resolving this disparity of treatment, which was manifestly unfair (Martin 2011; Boucoyannis 2013; Fleischacker 2013: 493–498). Class inequality, which was not only acceptable but as it should be (Hill 2016: 335),[26] was one thing, but inequality before the law was quite another. The latter, he said, 'is a form of oppression, and low wages are iniquitous' (Bhanu Mehta 2006: 257). According to his analysis, 'it is unjust for the state to harm the interests of some for no other purpose than to benefit another class of citizens, and thereby create inequality'; for this reason, he condemns virtually all policies that exacerbate inequality; obviously these unjust policies include 'laws permitting employers to combine' (Anderson 2016: 158, 159).[27]

---

[25]As he himself noted: 'Is this improvement in the circumstances of the lower ranks of the people to be regarded as an advantage or as an inconveniency to the society? The answer seems at first sight abundantly plain. Servants, labourers and workmen of different kinds, make up the far greater part of every great political society. But what improves the circumstances of the greater part can never be regarded as an inconveniency to the whole. No society can surely be flourishing and happy, of which the far greater part of the members are poor and miserable. It is but equity, besides, that they who feed, cloath and lodge the whole body of the people, should have such a share of the produce of their own labour as to be themselves tolerably well fed, cloathed and lodged' (Smith 1976, I.viii.36: 96). Not surprisingly, this passage has caused Smith to be seen as a champion of the workers and the poor (Fleischacker 2005: 66; McLean 2006: 140). But, on the other hand, his concern for the poor was always balanced by his passion for order (Hill 2016: 335). This aspect was underlined nearly a century ago by Viner (1927). For the multiple implications of this passage from the *Wealth of Nations* on poverty and for a less linear reading which restores some of Smith's ambiguity, see Martin (2015).

[26]In fact, 'the wise legislator respects the delicate concatenation of social and historical forces that have brought existing arrangements into being insensibly and by degrees' (Hill 2016: 331). Also, on Smith's ambiguity about natural tendencies within the structure of capitalism, see Fairlamb (1996: 193–223, especially 207–209).

[27]A similar remark was made by Lisa Hill, who wrote: 'he [Smith] seems to be suggesting that both [masters and workers] should desist from the practice and that the state should

Smith was fully aware that workers would never succeed in neutralising the offensive actions of the masters, which were far more effective than their own (Rubin 1979: 205–206).[28] He envisioned only two possible ways of correcting the existing violation of the principle of equality: one would be to allow workers recourse to the same weapons as the capitalists; and the other was to ensure that employers were pursued by the law in the same way that the state was harassing workers at the time. Smith left it to his readers to draw their own conclusions. Although he did not state it explicitly, it was clear from the way he framed the issue that, even if Parliament were to legislate in this sense and extend the treatment that had always been applied to workers to capitalists as well, it would in practice be next to impossible to discipline their strategies, chiefly because, as he emphasised, the agreements of capitalists were tacit rather than formally concluded and thus invisible and difficult to demonstrate, let alone punish.

For all their ambiguity, Smith's considerations raised at least three questions. Firstly, would allowing the workers recourse to the same weapons as the employers actually release wages from this trap (Stirati 1994: 51; Magnusson 2004: 25) and restore vitality to the mechanism of competition? Secondly, was this essentially just another example of Smith's profound scepticism of politics—and legislation in particular—for its inability to establish a fair set of rules, and of the state (namely, justice) regarding the exercise of its role as referee in ensuring respect for the rules of the game, such as they were?[29] Thirdly, could the market cure itself anyway, despite its being severely compromised by strategies that

---

stop colluding with masters' (Hill 2020: 133). As has been highlighted by Noell (1995: 229, 238), Smith 'did not recommend that Parliament should be concerned only with combinations of employers. In fact he opposed laws forbidding combinations of either type', believing 'that legislation should treat individuals and groups impartially, regardless of their position in the labour market'. The theme of inequality, more generally, is addressed by Lisa Hill (2020: ch. 5).

[28] According to Fleischacker (2004: 248–249) the workers were weaker than the capitalists but more aware of where their interests lay. For a different view, see Rothschild and Sen (2006: 328).

[29] On Smith's scepticism about public intervention: Forbes (1975: 180) and Coase (1976: 544). Both follow the classical study by Halévy (1928). Donald Winch (1978: 182) writes: 'Judged by its view of the motives, ambitions, and pretensions of political actors, Smith's politics was sceptical, pessimistic, or realistic, according to the reader's taste'.

tampered with competitive mechanisms? Even though workers' combinations were sure to be less effective than those of bosses, and perhaps it could not be otherwise, Smith did not imagine that wage levels could be regulated by political intervention on the state's part. History taught that laws aimed at balancing the interests of the workers and those of the employers always ended up favouring the latter. As he put it:

> Whenever the legislature attempts to regulate the differences between masters and their workmen, its counsellors are always the masters. When the regulation, therefore, is in favour of the workmen, it is always just and equitable; but it is sometimes otherwise when in favour of the masters. (Smith 1976, I.x.c.61: 157–158)

It was not the role of the state as such that Smith distrusted. No one subsequently has ever doubted that he foresaw the need for government intervention in certain circumstances. What he feared was the use that vested interests might be able to make of such intervention.[30] What Smith said to his students during a lecture he gave in February 1763 has become well known:

> Laws and government may be considered in this and indeed in every case as a combination of the rich to oppress the poor, and preserve to themselves the inequality of the goods which would otherwise be soon destroyed by the attacks of the poor, who if not hindered by the government would soon reduce the others to an equality with themselves by open violence. The government and laws hinder the poor from ever acquiring the wealth by violence, which they would otherwise exert on the rich; they tell them they must either continue poor or acquire wealth in the same manner as they have done. (Smith 1978, Report of 1762–3, iv.23: 208–209)[31]

[30]As Heinz Lubasz (1995: 53) has emphasised, 'Dugald Stewart was one distinguished political economist who saw clearly that the direct object of Smith's attack was not government policy but private vested interest'. In his *Account of the Life and Writings of Adam Smith*, presented to the Royal Society of Edinburgh in 1793, three years after Smith's death, he explained how—according to Smith—certain private interests had so heavily influenced economic policy as to create a system, but 'a false system of political economy, propagated by merchants and manufacturers; a class of individuals, whose interest is not always the same with that of the public, and whose professional knowledge gave them many advantages' (Stewart 1980: 316).

[31]On this passage, see the reflections by Rasmussen (2008: 71–76).

All legislative process was by its nature exposed to corruption (Hill 2006, 2020: ch. 5); and all interested parties, whether individual or collective, were naturally and inevitably seduced by the idea of approaching as closely as possible, and not always innocently, those involved in that process (Dickinson 1994: ch. 2).[32] To make his argument clearer, and to get back to the basic issue of conflicts of interest, Smith took the example of tailors and their relations with their own workers when it came to wages. This time, he introduced a few divergences from his earlier observations:

> Particular acts of Parliament, however, still attempt sometimes to regulate wages in particular trades and in particular places. Thus the 8th of George III [1768] prohibits under heavy penalties all master taylors in London, and five miles round it, from giving, and their workmen from accepting, more than two shilling and seven-pence halfpenny a day, except in the case of a general mourning. … [This act] is in favour of the masters. When masters combine together in order to reduce the wages of their workmen, they commonly enter into a private bond or agreement, not to give more than a certain wage under a certain penalty. Were the workmen to enter into a contrary combination of the same kind, not to accept of a certain wage under a certain penalty, the law would punish them very severely; and if it dealt impartially, it would treat the masters in the same manner. But the 8th of George III enforces by law that very regulation which masters sometimes attempt to establish by such combinations. The complaint of the workmen, that it puts the ablest and most industrious upon the same footing with an ordinary workman, seems perfectly well founded. (Smith 1976, I.x.c.61: 157–158)

[32] In particular as regards Smith's concerns over the pressure interest groups could exert over policy and the legislative activities of parliament, see Dickinson (1994: 59, 68). Besides, 'Smith's main purpose in writing about corruption was to confront and criticize the corrupt yet legal norms of the elite classes, norms that enabled them to exploit and control those in the lower orders and, in the long run, undermine the prosperity of the nation' (Hill 2006: 651). More generally in Smith's view, corruption 'consists in violations of the system of natural liberty, including violations that corrupt the naturally self-governing behaviour of individual actors' (Hill 2020: 130).

Wages, then, were a long way from being the outcome of a competitive mechanism that pitted the masters against one another in procuring the best men and constrained them to negotiate working conditions. To avoid that very competition, masters were given to uniting and abiding by pacts or private agreements with the scope of not giving more than a certain wage on pain of a forfeit. If the workers were to do the same, Smith said—to get together in an opposing combination and to refuse to accept less than a certain wage, on pain of some forfeit—they would be punished with the utmost severity. He then added something that he had not said previously: if the law were impartial, it ought to treat employers in the same way as the workers. And that wasn't all: in the case in question—that of the tailors—by positing a ceiling above which wages might not be agreed upon, the state was merely giving legal sanction to what the employers normally achieved through their conspiratorial behaviour. In other words, the market was doubly threatened: by the conspirators who manoeuvred in the shadows and by pressure groups who resorted, more or less openly, to politics in order to promote their own interests (Schmidtz 2016: 212–213).[33]

Finally, there was a third new element that Smith put before his readers. After drawing attention to the permeability and malleability of political action, which was inevitably partisan, he was at pains to stress that conspiratorial practices, which in the preceding section he had described as being the result of tacit agreements, sometimes stemmed from actual pacts and private arrangements. This put the matter in a slightly different light. Clearly, the way in which a fledgling capitalism had tampered with the game, tilting the conflict of interest between workers and employers irredeemably in the latter's favour, gave rise to two crucial questions: the first had to do with the principle of equality, the second with the principle of justice. While taking care not to call for legislative action to establish a political criterion for acceptably resolving the conflict of interest (Viner 1927: 214–215), Smith did not refrain from grasping the—no less political—thrust of how to safeguard the two principles. His idea

---

[33]As highlighted by Eric Schlisser (2017: 204–205), in these cases ('Masters are always and everywhere in a sort of tacit, but constant and uniform combination...' and 'Whenever the legislature attempts to regulate the differences between masters and their workmen, its counsellors are always the masters'), 'Smith offers universal generalizations'.

that workers should have the option to engage in their own conspiratorial action gave rise to a third issue that put the right to resist back on the table. This right derived *its* legitimacy from the necessity of safeguarding yet another principle: that of liberty. Once the scenario of tampering with the competition had been acknowledged and once it was understood that politics was at best incapable (and at worst corrupt), it was best to imagine fighting fire with fire. Even so, Smith did not conceal his pessimism, while avoiding anything that could lay him open to accusations of bad faith in imagining this realistic solution. It was implausible to envisage the workers' claims prevailing even in a conflict on theoretically equal terms. At the same time, it could not be completely ruled out that, in the long term, the social outcomes of the nascent industrial revolution and a future of freer trade might change things.[34]

According to Smith, in the American colonies—where growth at that time was exponential—conspiratorial strategies had not taken root. Unlike England, America had a labour market where employers, instead of uniting behind covert agreements, were in competition with one another to corner manpower that was still rather scarce.

Indeed, Smith writes:

> When in any country the demand for those who live by wages; labourers, journeymen, servants of every kind, is continually increasing; when every year furnishes employment for a greater number than had been employed the year before, the workmen have no occasion to combine in order to raise their wages. The scarcity of hands occasions a competition among masters, who bid against one another, in order to get workmen, and thus voluntarily break through the natural combination of masters not to raise wages. (Smith 1976, I.viii.17: 86)[35]

[34]'Smith thought the fruits of free trade would serve to diminish many of those conflicts between masters and workmen, but he also made it clear that economic growth would benefit the two parties in significantly different ways' (Teichgraeber 1986: 164). Similar observations had already been made by Samuel Hollander (1973: 185–187).

[35]'The demand for those who live by wages, it is evident, cannot increase but in proportion to the increase of the funds which are destined for the payment of wages. These funds are of two kinds; first, the revenue which is over and above what is necessary for the maintenance; and secondly, the stock which is over and above what is necessary for the employment of their masters. The demand for those who live by wages, therefore, necessarily increases with the increase of the revenue and stock of every country, and cannot possibly increase without it. The

Smith seemed sure. But it wasn't like that. It wasn't true that in America combinations between masters didn't exist because the labour force was still very small relative to the requirements of a still-young industry, or because the competition to get hold of the few workers available stifled at birth any possible conspiratorial agreement. Just as it wasn't true that, given these circumstances, the workers were not forced to defend themselves with the weapon of combination or that they were not stimulated to resort to it. In America, combinations between masters were widespread. They were sporadic, not systematic as in England, but they were an acknowledged reality. Unlike in England, these were not 'offensive' forms of conspiracy to keep wage levels down; they tended rather to be 'defensive', aimed at preventing wages rising too much. Exactly as Smith said, in America the number of workers was small compared to the demands of a rapidly growing industrial context, so that demand for labour kept the wage levels up. This fact not infrequently led the businessmen to come to agreements 'to set wage scales' (Morris 1937: 73). Consequently it cannot be said that, although it was a world of exceptional and unrivalled economic growth, it was also immune from conflict. Even in America, the sphere of wage-setting was not free from tension; this was a logical outcome of the interests in play, which were frequently protected by recourse to conspiratorial strategies.[36] A case that is in some ways remarkable took place in New York in 1785, when one combination was used to thwart another. The trouble broke out when the shoemakers went on strike to obtain higher wages from their masters. The masters responded by banding together in a counter-conspiracy to deny the requested wage rise, also demanding that the workers accept an agreement whereby they were bound to refuse any offer of work from

increase of revenue and stock is the increase of national wealth. The demand for those who live by wages, therefore, naturally increases with the increase of national wealth, and cannot possibly increase without it. It is not the actual greatness of national wealth, but its continual increase, which occasions a rise in the wages of labour. It is not, accordingly, in the richest countries, but in the most thriving, or in those which are growing rich the fastest, that the wages of labour are highest. England is certainly, in the present times, a much richer country than any part of North America. The wages of labour, however, are much higher in North America than in any part of England' (Smith 1976, I.viii.17: 86–87).

[36]However, the conspiratorial activities of the masters were hardly ever judicially pursued. As Richard B. Morris (1937: 73) states, 'the absence of prosecution of masters' combinations is especially characteristic of the prerevolutionary period'.

the retailers of British shoes. Initially the workers refused to accept these terms, but in the end, 'after a strike lasting over three weeks and during the most severe season of the year', they had to give in; when it had all blown over, 'the employers took back the workers at the old rates' (Morris 1937: 84–85).[37]

More generally, beyond this specific case and beyond what Smith was unaware of, from the mid-eighteenth century the phenomenon of the combinations began to take hold in many American cities, especially during the period of the Revolution. These were combinations of merchants, manufacturers and people belonging to generic 'occupational groups'. After having been used to combat and boycott the commercial policies imposed by the mother country, the weapon of combination was never definitively returned to the arsenal. As interests gradually became better defined and stronger they came to embody specific claims, both as protection against unforeseen and as yet ungoverned dynamics of change and so as to impose their own rationale when—after casting off the British yoke—American society began to reorganise itself and take stock of its strong points (Morris 1937: 72–78).

But the world that Smith had before him seemed so completely different that he saw the only way of preventing the workers being quashed by the power of the masters was to allow them to use the same weapons. Even if they were to remain hemmed in by the new power relations generated by capitalism, fighting fire with fire was certainly their only hope of keeping sight—in the broader sphere of justice—of three inalienable principles: equality, the right of defence or resistance and economic liberty. From the standpoint of political pragmatism or pessimism (Rasmussen 2014), if the idea that the law of the land would come to their rescue had to be abandoned, it was all the more necessary to guarantee equality of treatment on both fronts, to defend the natural right to protect life and limb, family and property, and at the same time safeguard the freedom of every individual to directly negotiate remuneration for his or her work, without constraint and in whatever way they thought best.

[37]As Richard B. Morris (1937: 84–85) points out, in America too approaches similar to those adopted in Britain were followed. While a certain tolerance was shown towards the combinations of masters, the attitude towards those organised by the workers was punitive and disciplinary.

And if the worker was penalised by having to conduct such a negotiation with an employer who was in tacit or explicit league with other potential employers, he or she was no less penalised by a wage ceiling that forced everyone, even the hardest-working, to submit to the same flat remuneration level as the idlest. In either case, Smith thought protest to be 'perfectly well founded' (Smith 1976, I.x.c.61: 158).

The issue of equality led on to a right of defence/resistance underwritten by the need to protect, first and foremost, the 'system of natural liberty'. Here too, however, the resistance of workers is still conceived from a strictly conservative viewpoint: it is aimed at halting and neutralising a violent state of affairs and is thus a response to a violation of the rules of the market by the capitalists. There was no question of justifying the opening of hostilities in the name of a utopian project, or of some hazy and impracticable overturning of the political structure. Workers are not in any sense imagined as active instruments of change. The collective strength deriving from their association is to be deployed in a conspiratorial manner only to defend and reinstate a violated order, an order that was at once moral and economic. And these were the two elements—the violation of the proper order of things and the exercise of the right to resist—that framed the issue in openly political terms.

Leaving aside Smith's explicit and peremptory denouncement, his argument was ambiguous regarding exactly what—in the event of political intervention of some kind—was expected to restore a framework of equality and guarantee the denied natural rights. And that wasn't the only ambiguity. The very choice of the words used to describe the conflict about wage definition certainly didn't help the reader to completely understand the very hazy dynamics in play and the actions that drove them. Even the adverbs used to illustrate the movement of the opposing parties seemed to cast a fairly weak light on the nature of the dispute. It appeared almost as if Smith wanted to portray it as a process that had been emptied of its voluntaristic essence in relation to the subjects involved. Was it plausible to portray such a conflict without assigning to the actors (i.e. the groups) a role that factored in solidarity and the cooperative dimension?

If indeed, as believed (Hill and Montag 2015: 142–146), what encourages men to interact is the pursuit of private interest, the logical consequence is that aggregation can only emerge within a strictly contractual context. In other words, cooperation cannot give rise to any social body except through agreements between subjects for the fulfilment of individually pursued interests. Therefore there are no forms of association outside the contractual dimension. Put in these terms, what emerges is a somewhat extravagant vision of human nature, albeit necessary to explain the functioning of the market in a certain manner.

Taken as a test bench for such an interpretation, the employers-workers scenario does effectively appear as a context in which the cooperative dimension is only apparent and somewhat blurry, and the wage bargaining triggered by the opposition of social entities cannot be expressed in collective terms. Let's take a look at the specific terms that have led to this reading. The capitalists are *tacitly* bound by an agreement that no one has signed, the result of which is to keep wages down. Consequently there is no interaction, no premeditation and no strategy. On the other side, all the workers do is resist, *violently*, in a disorderly and desperate manner. Their action is anything but organised, being stimulated purely by survival. It is simply a reaction to intolerable working and living conditions so that there is nothing considered, planned or shared about it. The tacit adherence to agreement, on the one hand, and spontaneous violence on the other, are precisely the opposite of cooperation understood as the lucid and conscious pursuit of a declared strategy for the achievement of a common goal. But there's something else too, and again it is the words used by Smith that urge us to consider another reading.

Beyond the *tacit* adherence to an agreement on the part of the masters, Smith's reasoning clearly shows that they are dually prompted to collaboration. Firstly, to fulfil their own individual interests, inseparable from those of the others and, secondly, to obtain the social approval of their 'neighbours and equals'. The reproach of those among the masters who did not want the implicit agreement to be foiled by violation was a form of social sanction that was ultimately welded to the interests of every one of them.

There are two other terms that Smith used to denote the action of the workers which stand out very clearly: *defence* and *resistance*, as I have already stressed. These two words indicate two forms of action that necessarily assume complicity. Not accepting wages below a certain level during the bargaining only has sense if it is done as a body. The mere refusal aimed at getting something more from the employer is cogent only when he cannot replace the claimant worker with another willing to accept the wages offered. Consequently, the performance of this individual action is tantamount to participating in the implementation of a strategy, or at least subscribing—perhaps only implicitly—to a political approach that goes beyond the one-to-one relationship. On this point at least there is no ambiguity in Smith's words. Moreover, in drawing the reader's attention to the behaviour of the workers involved in the action, he does not dwell only on the exasperation caused by their intolerable conditions. It does not appear to be mere blind violence unleashed as a purely instinctive response to oppression. In fact, at the very beginning of this reflection Smith explains to the reader how hard it is for the workers to uphold their interests in the dispute with the masters, precisely as a result of the paltry resources at their disposal. For the majority of them, it was practically impossible to hold out without wages for anything more than a week, with the result that such resistance was frequently insufficient to offset the effects of the implicit strategy the masters were involved in; at best, it could only attenuate them. In the end, resistance was much less effective and for this reason too—as well as being illegal—it tended every so often to alter its appearance and morph into a clamorous organised form. This was the only way the workers had 'to bring the point to a speedy decision'. In other words, they had no alternative. Finally, there were two other—anything but marginal—elements that appeared to confirm this reasoning. Firstly, the agitated and clamorous attitude of the workers was triggered by recourse to the weapon of combination in actions that were alternatively 'offensive' or 'defensive', but were in any case driven by a cooperative approach. Secondly, every so often the masters too gave in to disorderly action, especially in reaction to the workers' protests, and 'upon these occasions are just as clamorous upon the other side'. In sum, whether tacit or explicit, noisy or secret, the complicity of both masters and workers took place through actions characterised by solidarity.

Notwithstanding all this, it would be going too far to say that the reality Smith was talking about was moulded by collective actions. At least not yet. And Smith does not appear to have imagined the political effects his words would have. Nevertheless, although there were no well-defined, organised groups, clearly detectable on both sides was a complicity pregnant with social mechanisms and, above all, with conflict. The inherently cooperative conspiratorial rationale—the hub of the issue—was alive and kicking and its effects were evident and undeniable: low wages; disapproval of any violation of the masters' tacit agreements; workers sent to trial through 'the assistance of the civil magistrate' and 'the rigorous execution of those laws'.

Markets Besieged by Combinations

Once we digest Smith's ambiguous ruminations, and when we imagine the world through eighteenth-century liberal eyes, we see a society driven by individual interests and the market as a system for harmonising them and distributing resources 'equitably'. Needless to say, each person will get his or her fair share only if everyone is prepared to operate within a generally shared moral horizon, while competition will fulfil its function only so long as the state is able to guarantee a firm legal and moral framework. In reality, when speaking of the labour market Smith shows that, rather than being harmonised by a market driven by competition, the various interests can equally stand in opposition, play an associative role and become a source of conflict. At the same time, he proposes a solution to such an eventuality, undoubtedly less rosy and edifying, but just as free—from a liberal perspective—of the political legislative dimension. This alternative formula can nonetheless ensure the survival of the market, as well as its self-sufficiency. In this second scenario, individual interests no longer dominate, but sectors of society express their collective interest; there is no longer a market governed by an efficient mechanism that can harmonise these interests, but a market driven by a mechanism that actually feeds on conflict. That said, society maintains its autonomy from politics through self-organisation. In place of harmonisation by a natural dynamic, individual interests are aggregated into a collective interest and ranged against one another; groups are constrained to bargain, using the same immoral and illegal weapons, for whatever they can manage to extract from their 'enemies'. Any group tempted by a conspiratorial argument will sooner or later find its path blocked by its own victims, armed with the same reprehensible weaponry, and justified in its use by virtue of the principle of defence/resistance. This principle allows society to organise itself independently of politics (while adhering to another moral code), and the market to defend itself against the congenital pathology that renders it vulnerable to the ever-present menace of conspiracies aimed at perverting its natural functioning. After all, according to Smith, not only is conflict omnipresent (Bhanu Mehta 2006: 257), but the associative/conspiratorial propensity is as pervasive as it is ineradicable:

> People of the same trade seldom meet together, even for merriment and diversion, but the conversation ends in a conspiracy against the publick, or in some contrivance to raise prices. It is impossible indeed to prevent such meetings, by any law which either could be executed, or would be consistent with liberty and justice. But though the law cannot hinder people of the same trade from sometimes assembling together, it ought to do nothing to facilitate such assemblies; much less to render them necessary. (Smith 1976, I.x.c.27: 145)

Shortly after tackling the subject of a conflict of interest between masters and workers, and shortly before returning to it and highlighting the legislative disparity of treatment and frequent bias in the employers' favour, Smith addresses the conspiratorial menace hanging over the market in more general but no less revealing terms. This tendency on the part of society to foment conspiracies more or less naturally seems to him a blind spot. The state, to be sure, has no business encouraging associative/conspiratorial tendencies, nor rendering them easy, still less necessary to concoct. Any aggregation is—or could become—a threat to the market and to other interests. This begs an obvious question: would society be better off remaining, as it were, unaggregated, would it be better for conflicting interests to remain fragmentary?

It was definitely conceivable that competition might function better, and the market succeed better in harmonising interests, if the latter retained their individuality. It was nevertheless hard to believe, and Smith was indeed pessimistic. On the other hand, it was just as unrealistic to suppose that the state could prevent conspiratorial outbreaks as it was difficult to see how it could prove or penalise them. Smith's pragmatism in this sphere was tied into an important aspect of his conception of natural liberty. Any state action aimed at disciplining combinations conflicted with certain fundamental principles of justice, in the sense of curtailing the liberty of anyone wishing to band together, yoking the destiny of their own interests to that of others. This, too, was surely a natural and unassailable right, just like the right to trade. We should add that Smith 'wrote at a time when virtually all state interference with the *system of natural liberty* was on behalf of the rich. In that context the interests of market freedom and equality coincide' (Anderson 2016: 169).

Therefore, any attempt to discipline combinations would risk undermining society or rendering it vulnerable to power relations already well-established within it. After all, such conspiracies, while detrimental to the proper functioning of the competition mechanism, were generated by an aggregative impulse and were hence an obvious sign of the vitality of an increasingly commercial society. They were its lifeblood. As Smith himself pointed out, on any occasion when economic players gathered together for commercial or other reasons, their meetings were liable to turn into forms of complicity with the potential to become combinations.[38] He was well aware that it was the market itself which produced such complicity. What market was ever immune to the strategies of those who, in pursuit of their own interests, constantly sought accomplices to manipulate its trajectory? The problem, Smith insisted, was that such conspiratorial initiatives were almost always against the *public* interest.

---

[38]On the tension between Smith's confidence in the system of natural liberty and his polemics against combinations, see Turpin (2011: 43–45). In many passages, liberty seems to mean liberty of contract (Schlisser 2017: 216–220).

As we said, it was interests that ruled the world, and they never lied; they moved the hearts of individuals and determined their actions. On the other hand, as Smith insistently pointed out, it was impossible to deny that the pursuit of these interests frequently led to social groupings that threatened the harmony of the community. Moreover, what were the conspiracies if not factions of an economic nature that disturbed the natural course of the market?

The conspiratorial dimension that materialised in the form of the combination was none other than the reflection of a factionary mentality. This derived both from men's desire to be appreciated and recognised (Brubaker 2006: 184) and from their intention to pursue their own advantage in collusion with others so as to sidestep the challenges of competition. The example of the masters illustrated perfectly the diabolical dovetailing of these two mechanisms; the faction was the germ of a social disease, a major threat to both the survival of the market and the maintenance of civil and political order (Levy and Peart 2009: 335, 337). Its very mode of action contradicted the moral bonds underlying the framework of trust that held together both the market and society as a whole.

There was, however, a twist that had eluded Smith—or that he barely glimpsed—that was later highlighted by one of his pupils, the legal philosopher John Millar. If men are naturally inclined to conspire to divert the flow of the market in their favour, surely they must be no less 'naturally' moved—by an analogous commercial impulse—to interact with one another to resist that process and develop mutual defence resources:

> The spirit of liberty appears, in commercial countries, to depend chiefly upon two circumstances: first, the condition of the people relative to the distribution of property, and the means of subsistence; secondly, the facility with which the several members of society are enabled to associate and to act in concert with one another. (Millar 1960: 330–331)[39]

[39]On the connections between the expansion of commerce and industry and the elimination of arbitrary and authoritarian decision-making by the sovereign, I refer to the pages on Montesquieu, Steuart and Millar by Albert O. Hirschman (1977: 70–93). In the case of a *grand coup d'autorité* (tyrannical action), Hirschman writes, 'the situation could still be saved if there

As Albert Hirschman has noted, Millar was fully persuaded that the development of commerce and manufacture had been, and continued to be, one of the main driving forces behind the spread of the spirit of liberty, and he was no less convinced that this development had boosted and made viable the ability 'of certain social groups to resort to collective action against oppression and mismanagement' (Hirschman 1977: 89). This spirit provided an antidote to both the potential political threat of tyrannical action and the threat posed by conspiratorial tendencies infesting the market. Therefore, the market would be able to survive its own destructive forces if subjects had a chance to defend themselves by conspiring against the conspirators. Any monopolistic strategy would hence become a victim of its victim, in a dynamic whereby every form of pathology was neutralised by the antidote it naturally produced.

As Donald Winch wrote:

> Smith's interest lay in counterbalancing the power possessed by masters. The best solution might be one in which all forms of combination were outlawed; but on this, as on most legislative matters, Smith was not content to confine himself to ideal conditions. In an imperfect world, counterbalancing an existing imbalance constituted the best course of action from the point of view of both expediency and justice. (Winch 1996: 204)

This was at once a surrender and a wager.[40] It was a relation of power in which opposing interests were pursued through conspiracy. There was also the risk that the new market that was emerging from capitalist culture would establish a dynamic far removed from the tried and tested competitive mechanism. Was trusting to the countervailing of forces that

---

were forces in the society that would rapidly mobilize to oppose the prince and make him retract or modify his policies. What was needed was a feedback or equilibrating mechanism that would restore conditions favorable to the expansion of commerce and industry should they be disturbed' (1977: 88). On this topic, see also Haakonssen (1996: 165–166).

[40]As underscored by Noell (1995: 229), 'Smith's recommended policy of neutrality towards economic combinations stemmed from his opposition towards exclusive privilege in general [...] there is in fact a linkage between this opposition and Smith's reliance upon the concept of commutative justice [...] Smith and the scholastics shared a distrust of different forms of labor market combination. Unlike the scholastics, however, Smith explicitly denied the efficacy and justice of laws which prohibited the formation of labor market combinations'.

were formally and inherently threatening truly the only way of thwarting them?

This apparently new dynamic offered a faint glimpse of a phenomenon that was not exactly foreign to the markets but that little was known about.[41] The features of a moral and judicial solution that had been widely debated in Europe up to little more than a century earlier were instead distinctly recognisable. Although it appeared to have vanished without trace, this was not the case at all. In its original form this solution had been conceived, more generically, to offset the opposing and conspiratorially organised interests of buyers and sellers. But the rationale was essentially the same (Lubasz 1995: 58).[42] Therefore it is very likely that, without being fully aware of it, Smith had resuscitated the old principle whereby it was morally and legally justified, as well as inevitable and necessary, to thwart a monopolistic conspiracy (such as that of the masters) by resorting to the same weapons as the conspirators. In other words, the markets would achieve self-sufficiency and immortality through the mechanism of *monopolium vs. monopolium.* All Smith had done was to find in the new context of capitalist society a formidable application for an idea originally elaborated in theological circles and then taken over by the legal world between the sixteenth and seventeenth centuries. In actual fact, he did more than that: by restyling that old precept which deemed it just to withstand one monopoly with another he opened a breach, allowing the classical economists to turn it into a sort of corollary of the liberal notion of free market. In this way, there was no longer any need to be afraid of a world populated by giants because their potentially tyrannical strength would prove to be harmless.

---

[41]The process of counterbalancing would trigger naturally, as was to be explained later and as, in actual fact, had already been explained at least a century before by Jacques Savary, a French jurist particularly attentive to the dynamics animating the markets. See ch. 3.

[42]'In this respect workers and masters don't differ from other sellers and buyers in a market' (Lubasz 1995: 58).

References

Alvey, J.E. 2003. *Adam Smith: Optimist or Pessimist? A New Problem Concerning the Teleological Basis of Commercial Society*. Aldershot: Taylor & Francis.

Anderson, E. 2016. Adam Smith on Equality. In *Adam Smith. His Life, Thought, and Legacy*, ed. R.P. Hanley, 157–172. Princeton, NJ and Oxford: Princeton University Press.

Bhanu Mehta, P. 2006. Self-Interest and Other Interests. In *The Cambridge Companion to Adam Smith*, ed. K. Haakonssen, 246–269. Cambridge and New York: Cambridge University Press.

Boucoyannis, D. 2013. The Equalizing Hand: Why Adam Smith Thought the Market Should Produce Wealth Without Steep Inequality. *Perspectives on Politics* 11 (4): 1051–1070.

Braudel, F. 1977. *Afterthoughts on Material Civilisation and Capitalism*. Baltimore: John Hopkins University Press.

Brubaker, L. 2006. Does the 'Wisdom of Nature' Need Help? In *New Voices on Adam Smith*, ed. L. Montes and E. Schlisser, 168–192. London and New York: Routledge.

Clark, C.M.A. 1988. Natural Law Influences on Adam Smith. *Quaderni di Storia dell'Economia Politica* 6 (3): 59–86.

Coase, R.H. 1976. Adam Smith's View of Man. *Journal of Law and Economics* 19 (3): 529–546.

Cohen, E.S. 1989. Justice and Political Economy in Commercial Society: Adam Smith's 'Science of a Legislator'. *The Journal of Politics* 51 (1): 50–72.

Cremaschi, S. 1989. Adam Smith. Skeptical Newtonianism, Disenchanted Republicanism, and the Birth of Social Science. In *Knowledge and Politics: Case Studies on the Relationship Between Epistemology and Political Philosophy*, ed. M. Dascal and O. Gruengard, 83–110. Boulder, CO: Westview.

Dickinson, H.T. 1994. *The Politics of the People in Eighteenth-Century Britain*. New York: St. Martin's Press.

Elliott, J.E. 2000. Adam Smith's Conceptualization of Power, Markets and Politics. *Review of Social Economy* 58 (4): 429–454.

Evensky, J. 2005a. *Adam Smith's Moral Philosophy. A Historical and Contemporary Perspective on Markets, Law, Ethics, and Culture*. Cambridge: Cambridge University Press.

Evensky, J. 2005b. Adam Smith's 'Theory of Moral Sentiments': On Morals and Why They Matter to a Liberal Society of Free People and Free Markets. *The Journal of Economic Perspectives* 19 (3): 109–130.

Fairlamb, H.L. 1996. Smith's Other Hand: A Capitalist Theory of Exploitation. *Social Theory and Practice* 22 (2): 193–223.
Fleischacker, S. 2004. *On Adam Smith's Wealth of Nations. A Philosophical Companion*. Princeton, NJ and Oxford: Princeton University Press.
Fleischacker, S. 2005. *A Short History of Distributive Justice*. Cambridge, MA and London: Harvard University Press.
Fleischacker, S. 2013. Adam Smith on Equality. In *Oxford Handbook of Adam Smith*, ed. C.J. Berry, M.P. Paganelli, and C. Smith, 485–500. Oxford: Oxford University Press.
Forbes, D. 1975. Sceptical Whiggism, Commerce and Liberty. In *Essays on Adam Smith*, ed. A.S. Skinner and T. Wilson, 179–201. Oxford: Clarendon Press.
Force, P. 2003. *Self-Interest Before Adam Smith. A Genealogy of Economic Science*. Cambridge and New York: Cambridge University Press.
Galbraith, J.K. 1956 [1952]. *American Capitalism. The Concept of Countervailing Power*. Harmondsworth: Penguin.
Haakonssen, K. 1981. *The Science of Legislator. The Natural Jurisprudence of David Hume and Adam Smith*. Cambridge: Cambridge University Press.
Haakonssen, K. 1996. *Natural Law and Moral Philosophy. From Grotius to the Scottish Enlightenment*. Cambridge: Cambridge University Press.
Haakonssen, K. 2016. The Lectures on Jurisprudence. In *Adam Smith. His Life, Thought, and Legacy*, ed. R.P. Hanley, 48–66. Princeton, NJ and Oxford: Princeton University Press.
Halévy, E. 1928. *The Growth of Philosophic Radicalism*. London: Faber & Faber.
Hamowy, R. 1987. *The Scottish Enlightenment and the Theory of Spontaneous Order*. Carbondale and Edwardsville: Southern Illinois University Press.
Herzog, L. 2013a. *Inventing the Market. Smith, Hegel and Political Theory*. Oxford: Oxford University Press.
Herzog, L. 2013b. The Community of Commerce: Smith's Rhetoric of Sympathy in the Opening of the *Wealth of Nations*. *Philosophy and Rhetoric* 46 (1): 65–87.
Hill, J.E. 2016. *Adam Smith's Equality and the Pursuit of Happiness*. London and New York: Palgrave Macmillan.
Hill, L. 2006. Adam Smith and the Theme of Corruption. *Review of Politics* 68 (4): 636–662.
Hill, L. 2016. Adam Smith and Political Theory. In *Adam Smith: His Life, Thought, and Legacy*, ed. R.P. Hanley, 321–339. Princeton, NJ and Oxford: Princeton University Press.

Hill, L. 2020. *Adam Smith's Pragmatic Liberalism. The Science of Welfare*. London and New York: Palgrave Macmillan.
Hill, M., and W. Montag. 2015. *The Other Adam Smith*. Stanford: Stanford University Press.
Hirschman, A.O. 1977. *The Passions and the Interests. Political Arguments for Capitalism Before Its Triumph*. Princeton, NJ: Princeton University Press.
Hollander, S. 1973. *The Economics of Adam Smith*. London: Heinemann Educational Books; Toronto: University of Toronto Press.
Hume, D. 1752. *Political Discourses*. Edinburgh: Fleming.
Hutcheson, F. 1747. *A Short Introduction to Moral Philosophy in Three Books, Containing the Elements of Ethicks and the Law of Nature*. Glasgow: Foulis.
Hutcheson, F. 1755. *A System of Moral Philosophy in Three Books*, 2 vols. London: Foulis.
Ingham, G. 2008. *Capitalism*. Cambridge: Polity.
Kennedy, G. 2008. *Adam Smith. A Moral Philosopher and His Political Economy*. London and New York: Routledge.
Le Mercier de la Rivière, P.-P. 1767. *L'ordre naturel et essentiel des sociétés politiques*. London: Nourse.
Levy, D.M., and S. Peart. 2009. Adam Smith and the Place of Faction. In *Elgar Companion to Adam Smith*, ed. J.T. Joung, 335–345. Cheltenham: Edward Elgar.
Lubasz, H. 1995. Adam Smith and the 'Free Market'. In *Adam Smith's Wealth of Nations. New Interdisciplinary Essays*, ed. S. Copley and K. Sutherland. Manchester: Manchester University Press.
Magnusson, L. 2004. *The Tradition of Free Trade*. London and New York: Routledge.
Malcomson, R.W. 1984. Workers Combinations in Eighteenth-Century England. In *The Origins of Anglo-American Radicalism*, ed. M. Jacob and J. Jacob, 149–161. London, Boston, and Sydney: Allen & Unwin.
Martin, C. 2011. Adam Smith and Liberal Economics: Reading the Minimum Wage Debate of 1795–96. *Econ Journal Watch* 8 (2): 110–125.
Martin, C. 2015. Equity, Besides: Adam Smith and the Utility of Poverty. *Journal of the History of Economic Thought* 4: 559–581.
McLean, I. 2006. *Adam Smith, Radical and Egalitarian. An Interpretation for the Twenty-First Century*. Edinburgh: Edinburgh University Press.
McNulty, P.J. 1973. Adam Smith's Concept of Labor. *Journal of the History of Ideas* 34 (3): 345–366.

Millar, J. 1960 [1803]. The Advancement of Manufactures, Commerce, and the Arts, Since the Reign of William III; and the Tendency of This Advancement to Diffuse a Spirit of Liberty and Independence. In *John Millar of Glasgow, 1735–1801. His Life and Thought and His Contribution to Sociological Analysis*, ed. W.C. Lehmann, 326–333. Cambridge: Cambridge University Press.

Moher, J. 1988. From Suppression to Containment: Roots of Trade Union Law to 1825. In *British Trade Unionism, 1750–1850. The Formative Years*, ed. J. Rule, 74–97. London and New York: Longman.

Moore, J., and M. Silverthorne. 2002. Foreword. In *Natural Rights on the Threshold of the Scottish Enlightenment. The Writings of Gershom Carmichael*, ed. J. Moore and M. Silverthorne. Indianapolis: Liberty Fund.

Morris, R.B. 1937. Criminal Conspiracy and Early Labor Combinations in New York. *Political Science Quarterly* 52 (1): 51–85.

Necker, J. 1820a [1775]. *Sur la législation et le commerce de grains*. In *Œuvres complètes de Mr. Necker*, publiées par le baron de Staël, 15 vols., Tome I. Paris: Treuttel et Würtz.

Necker, J. 1820b [1784]. *De l'administration des finances de la France*. In *Œuvres complètes de Mr. Necker*, publiées par le baron de Staël, 15 vols., Tome V. Paris: Treuttel et Würtz.

Noell, E.S. 1995. Adam Smith on Economic Justice in the Labor Market. *Journal of the History of Economic Thought* 17 (2): 228–246.

Ogose, T. 2003. Morality, Polity and Economy in Francis Hutcheson. In *The Rise of Political Economy in the Scottish Enlightenment*, ed. T. Sakamoto and H. Tanaka, 39–54. London and New York: Routledge.

Orth, J.V. 1987. English Combination Acts of the Eighteenth Century. *Law and History Review* 5 (1): 175–211.

Orth, J.V. 1991. *Combination and Conspiracy. A Legal History of Trade Unionism, 1721–1906*. Oxford: Clarendon Press.

Pack, S.P. 1991. *Capitalism as a Moral System. Adam Smith's Critique of the Free Market Economy*. Cheltenham and Northampton, MA: Edward Elgar.

Perelman, M. 2000. *The Invention of Capitalism. Classical Political Economy and the Secret History of Primitive Accumulation*. Durham and London: Duke University Press.

Phelps Brown, E.H. 1976. The Labour Market. In *The Market and the State. Essays in Honour of Adam Smith*, ed. T. Wilson and A.S. Skinner, 243–259. Oxford: Clarendon Press.

Phillipson, N. 2010. *Adam Smith. An Enlightened Life*. New Haven, CT: Yale University Press.

Rasmussen, D.C. 2008. *The Problems and Promise of Commercial Society. Adam Smith's Response to Rousseau*. University Park, PA: The Pennsylvania State University Press.

Rasmussen, D.C. 2014. *The Pragmatic Enlightenment. Recovering the Liberalism of Hume, Smith, Montesquieu, and Voltaire*. Cambridge and New York: Cambridge University Press.

Ron, A. 2008. Modern Natural Law Meets the Market: The Case of Adam Smith. *European Journal of Political Economy* 7 (2): 117–136.

Rothschild, E. 2001. *Economic Sentiments. Adam Smith, Condorcet and the Enlightenment*. London and Cambridge, MA: Harvard University Press.

Rothschild, E., and A. Sen. 2006. Adam Smith's Economics. In *The Cambridge Companion to Adam Smith*, ed. K. Haakonssen, 319–365. Cambridge and New York: Cambridge University Press.

Rubin, I.I. 1979 [1929]. *A History of Economic Thought*. London: Ink Links.

Sandmo, A. 2016. Adam Smith and Modern Economics. In *Adam Smith: His Life, Thought, and Legacy*, ed. R.P. Hanley, 231–246. Princeton, NJ and Oxford: Princeton University Press.

Schlisser, E. 2017. *Adam Smith. Systematic Philosopher and Public Thinker*. Oxford and New York: Oxford University Press.

Schmidtz, D. 2016. Adam Smith on Freedom. In *Adam Smith. His Life, Thought, and Legacy*, ed. R.P. Hanley, 208–227. Princeton, NJ and Oxford: Princeton University Press.

Schmitt, C. 1976 [1932]. *The Concept of the Political*. New Brunswick: Rutgers University Press.

Schumpeter, J.A. 2006 [1954]. *History of Economic Analysis*. London and New York: Routledge.

Sen, A. 2011. Uses and Abuses of Adam Smith. *History of Political Economy* 43 (2): 257–271.

Sheehan, J., and D. Wahrman. 2015. *Invisible Hands. Self-Organization and the Eighteenth-Century*. Chicago and London: University of Chicago Press.

Smith, A. 1976 [1776]. *An Inquiry into the Nature and Causes of the Wealth of Nations*, 2 vols., ed. R.H. Campbell and A.S. Skinner. Oxford: Oxford University Press.

Smith, A. 1978. *Lectures on Jurisprudence*, ed. R.L. Meek, D.D. Raphael, and P.G. Stein. Oxford: Oxford University Press.

Stein, P. 1979. Adam Smith's Jurisprudence—Between Morality and Economics. *Cornell Law Review* 64 (4): 621–638.

Steuart, J. 1767. *An Inquiry into the Principles of Political Economy*, 2 vols. London: Millar & Cadell.

Stewart, D. 1980 [1794]. *Account of the Life and Writings of Adam Smith*, LL.D. In A. Smith, *Essays on Philosophical Subjects*, ed. W.P.D. Wightman and J.C. Bryce, 269–332. Oxford: Oxford University Press.

Stirati, A. 1994. *The Theory of Wages in Classical Economics. A Study of Adam Smith, David Ricardo and Their Contemporaries.* Aldershot and Brookfield: Edward Elgar.

Taylor, W.L. 1965. *Francis Hutcheson and David Hume as Predecessors of Adam Smith.* Durham: Duke University Press.

Teichgraeber, III, R.F. 1986. *'Free Trade' and Moral Philosophy. Rethinking the Sources of Adam Smith's Wealth of Nations.* Durham: Duke University Press.

Tucker, J. 1750. *A Brief Essay on the Advantages and Disadvantages Which Respectively Attend France and Great Britain with Regard to Trade.* London: Trye.

Turgot, A.R.J. 2011a [1766]. *Reflections on the Formation and Distribution of Wealth.* In *The Turgot Collection. Writings, Speeches, and Letters of Anne Robert Jacques Turgot, Baron de Laune*, ed. D. Gordon, 5–65. Auburn: Mises Institute.

Turpin, P. 2011. *The Moral Rhetoric of Political Economy. Justice and Modern Economic Thought.* London and New York: Routledge.

Viner, J. 1927. Adam Smith and Laissez-Faire. *Journal of Political Economy* 35 (2): 198–232.

Winch, D. 1978. *Adam Smith's Politics. An Essay on Historiographic Revision.* Cambridge: Cambridge University Press.

Winch, D. 1996. *Riches and Poverty. An Intellectual History of Political Economy in Britain, 1750–1834.* Cambridge: Cambridge University Press.

Young, J.T. 2005. Unintended Order and Intervention: Adam Smith's Theory of the Role of the State. *History of Political Economy* 37: 91–119.

Young, J.T. 2008. Law and Economics in the Protestant Natural Tradition: Samuel Pufendorf, Francis Hutcheson, and Adam Smith. *Journal of the History of Economic Thought* 30 (3): 283–296.

3

Monopoly Versus Monopoly

The Right to Resist Takes on a New Guise

Long before anyone had ever suggested that power might be checked (or defeated) only by a contrary power, it had been thought that the only way to defuse the passions was to set one against the other. These were the antidotes to the two greatest disasters facing Western civilisation. In one case, averting the threat of tyranny and saving political institutions and the state from annihilation; in the other, curbing the individual's tendency to indulge his or her basest instincts, which jeopardised coexistence, not to mention survival. Bacon and then Spinoza were the first to consider ways of stemming the passions and Montesquieu later investigated how to keep power from sliding into despotism. No doubt one of the proposed antidotes gave rise to the other (Hirschman 1977: 30).[1] And—*mirabile dictu*—the same line of reasoning had been deployed

[1]As Albert O. Hirschman puts it, 'it seems rather plausible that the former principle laid the intellectual groundwork for the principle of separation of powers' (1977: 30). For a critical reading of Hirschman's work, see Pierre Force (2003: ch. 4).

R. Rosolino, *Countervailing Powers*,
https://doi.org/10.1007/978-3-030-37802-8_3

many decades earlier to justify strategies of resistance that aimed to neutralise the dark forces that, in the markets (and elsewhere), threatened the dynamics whereby goods, once attributed a value, came to be exchanged.

Monopolies contained elements of both threats. Incarnations of the vice of untrammelled greed were implemented through the exercise of an essentially tyrannical power. They were the upshot of mankind's immoral tendency to love money and material possessions and of the violent, unconstrained exercise of economic strength, which was by nature politically threatening. They also posed a third, no less crucial, problem. Once it was proposed that the crime of monopoly—which was at once a sin and an offence—might be blocked by an equal and opposite force, it became common to think of it as something that generally originated in a breakdown of the rules of the game. In other words, being guilty of monopolistic activity implied that one was a threat to the fiduciary fabric of society, perhaps the chief bond holding society together. Nonetheless, it was considered admissible (and necessary) to counteract an ongoing monopolistic conspiracy by enacting a no less reprehensible and damaging strategy.

The first person to come to this conclusion was the great Spanish Dominican Domingo de Soto, one of the leading exponents of the School of Salamanca, a pupil of the better-known Francisco de Vitoria (theoretician of the 'just war') and confessor to the Emperor Charles V. Soto formulated the following precept in his *De iustitia et iure*: 'There can be no doubt that when sellers form a monopoly, then buyers may legitimately have recourse to a contrary precaution, repelling as it were force with force: that is to say, agree between themselves that none among them will buy above a certain price' (Soto 1582: 196).[2]

A monopoly could be opposed by deploying an equal and opposite force.[3] The expression 'quasi vim vi repellentes' refers to the principle

[2]My translation of the following sentence: 'Quando verò venditores monopolium facerent, tunc iustè emptores, quasi vim vi repellentes contraria pariter possent prudentia uti: puta convenire inter se, ut nullus nisi certo pretio emeret' (Soto 1582: 196). This passage was noted, but only fleetingly, by Odd Langholm (1998: 98).

[3]Soto also made an important contribution to the Catholic development of the concept of the right of resistance: see Mario Turchetti (1999: 76–77).

of legitimate defence, a traditional tenet of Roman law.[4] However, in this case, although the logic was the same, the context diverged from the 'normal' circumstances in which sanctioning the use of force against force was necessary. The strategy was envisaged very much as a last resort, admissible only in the face of a particular situation. Its exact characteristics were still imprecise, and its application required prudence. Even so, from its earliest conception, its radicality and moral foundations were recognised. It would soon be reformulated as a necessary response when, faced by a hostile alignment of despotic nature, there was no alternative but to resort to the same violation of the pact on which the market was founded. To defend oneself against a monopoly was to *resist*.

Rather than being used in its strictest, that is, political, sense—as an exclusive privilege granted by the king or by some delegated authority—the term *monopoly* was applied to any kind of behaviour aimed at interfering with free bargaining in the marketplace. The category therefore embraced the majority of salient abuses from which the markets and those operating in them needed to be protected. The treatise writers of second scholasticism spoke of monopoly as an act of theft, of violence even, and as an offence against commutative justice insofar as it involved establishing an equivalence between the price and the value of the merchandise exchanged (Piotrowski 1933; Höffner 1941; De Roover 1974a; Langholm 1998: 94–99; 2006: 395–411; Prodi 2009: 86–87, 248–259). It was often indeed bracketed with usury, following Aristotle. Every murky or fraudulent means of manipulating exchange dynamics and, extending the net wider, any attempt to influence the process

[4]The first known statement of the *vim vi repellere licet* concept is to be found in Cicero's *Pro Milone*, 10, where it is held to derive directly from the human conscience, and is, in fact, an innate principle of natural law: 'Est igitur haec, iudices, non scripta, sed nata lex, quam non didicimus, accepimus, legimus, verum ex natura ipsa adripuimus, hausimus, expressimus, ad quam non docti sed facti, non istituti sed imbuti sumus, ut, si vita nostra in aliquas insidias, si in vim et in tela aut latronum aut inimicorum incidisset, omnis honesta ratio esset expediendae salutis'. The motto is then taken up by the jurist Cassius, according to a passage in Ulpiano's books on *ad edictum* in the *Digesta Iustiniani*: 'vim vi repellere licet Cassius scribit idque ius natura comparatur: apparet autem, inquit, ex eo arma armis repellere licet' (D. 43, 16, 1, 27); and is mentioned again in the *Digesta* by Paulus: 'vim enim vi defendere omnes leges omniaque jura permittunt' (D. 9, 2, 45, 4). Francisco de Vitoria also used the same expression in his *De iure belli* (1539), Quaestio prima: 'Et quia de bello defensivo revocari in dubium non potest, quia *vim vi repellere licet*' (ff. *De iustitia et iure*, l. *Ut vim*).

of ascribing value to goods and labour was labelled as a monopoly. Jurists used this word to describe the most diverse forms of complicity employed to distort normal transactions to the advantage of one party.[5] Monopolies were almost never the work of an individual, usually resulting from the manoeuvres of a group of speculators (Braudel 1982: 412–421). More precisely, these were *conventicule*,[6] behind which lurked perilous 'machinations' (Reginaldo 1616: II, 512–513). Being involved in such a thing lay one open to an accusation of 'conspiracy' (Piotrowski 1933: 187–189). And if from a moral and juridical point of view it made no difference whether such practices were the work of one or more hands, it seemed to make no difference either to those, such as Thomas More (2002: 19)[7] and Jean Bodin (1997: 68), who were concerned with emphasising political repercussions. For them too, monopolies were equivalent to agreements concocted between sellers or buyers

[5]In the summary of the famous jurist Prospero Farinacci a monopoly might relate to three things—goods, people or a particular place: 'Monopolium proprie committi dicitur inter plures mercatores seu artifices, quando inter se concordant, conspirant, & conveniunt ut omnes uno certo praetio vendant, & non minori [...] monopolium in mercibus, quando mercatores certum pretium inter se constituunt, & non alio pretio vendere velle conveniunt [...] monopolii crimen dixit incurrere eos, qui conveniunt non locare domus, vel apothecas, vel alia aedificia, aut bona, nisi tanto pretio [...] Monopolium committi dicitur, & illius poena locum habet, quando civitas aut tacite aut expresse, quod nullus rusticus debeat laborare in fundis forensium, aut illos ab iniuria pecorum defendere, seu juvare [...] Monopolium praecipue committitur, quando quis emit aliquam victualiae totam speciem, ut puta frumentum, vinum, oleum, & similia, ut is solus & unus vendendi potestatem habeat, & non alius [...] Monopolium committi dicitur non solum in mercibus, sed etiam in loco, ut puta, quando statuitur, quod pastilli aut alia victualia non vendantur, vel emantur, nisi in certo loco; [...] monopolium committere etiam eos, qui conveniunt, quod homines talis municipij non deferant frumentum, vel alias merces, in proximum municipium' (Farinacci 1621: 421–422). For another example, where this appears equally clear, see Schuster (1686: 18).

[6]That is, aggregations for nefarious purposes, to distinguish them from their opposite 'congregationes', convened for good ends (Tepati 1682: III, 385). See also Grassis (1617: 5): in the summary, point 4 is entitled *Amicitia ad malum non dicitur amicitia, sed conspiratio fraudis.*

[7]On the importance of this passage in *Utopia* by Thomas More, see Schumpeter (2006: 290–291): 'People were quite familiar with the pattern of monopoly, on wich they bestowed an impulsive hatred, and with competition, which they conceived to be the normal pattern without bothering to define it. But as early as 1516, it occurred to Sir Thomas More that for competition to prevail it is not necessarily sufficient that a commodity be sold by more than one seller. Prices may fail to fall to the competitive level also if sellers are few, *quod... si monopolium appellari non potest... certe oligopolium est.* Thus More introduced the concept of oligopoly'.

to sell or buy at a price higher or lower than that which might be naturally determined by the marketplace and could thus be seen as just. Monopolies and monopsonies were one and the same thing, and they fell under the same criminal category as both pacts between merchants aimed to create a fall or rise in current valuations and agreements among members of a given trade to provide their services only on certain terms. Even meddling with the correct conduct of an auction was considered *monopolium*.

The risk of being the victim of a monopolist's trap hovered like a spectre over the collective imagination of a society pervaded by uncertainty such as that of the *Ancien Régime* (Grenier 1996: 145–169, 299–321). And, of course, there was no famine that did not conceal the malign manoeuvrings of profiteers just as there was no price rise that was not the result of the dark designs of speculators: of those, that is, who manipulated the normal price-setting mechanisms through monopolistic procedures (Kaplan 1982, 1984).[8] For these mechanisms to operate in a free and spontaneous manner it was necessary that those exchanging, buying, and selling—or more broadly, any players in the game regardless of whether they directly participated in the exchange process—should not be guilty of either violence or fraud. Monopolies involved both. As Botero put it, they were the *outcome* of fraud. More specifically, 'knavery' makes less noise than violence, but is no less harmful; it restricts trading to monopolies and undermines 'the peace and harmony of the state' (Botero 1956: 20). This was why it was not just a question of practices that were detrimental to the life and proper functioning of the markets: their more menacing aspects threatened the very survival of the political order.[9]

So how, despite centuries of condemnation backed by an impressive volume of—mainly Franciscan and Dominican—theological and juridical treatises, did the idea come about that these dangerous conspiratorial practices might be best countered by the victims defending themselves with same arms as the conspirators? And did this not mark the moment

[8] More generally, a number of examples are cited in Ó Gráda (2009: ch. V).

[9] For another important example, I refer to Jean Duret (1583: 30*v*-32*v*; 119-*v*). On the attention paid by both Botero and Duret to this kind of speculative practices, see Maifreda (2012: 107–112).

at which the market came to be seen (both literally and metaphorically) as a site contended by menacing forces with patently monopolistic ambitions, but also, for all its essential fragility, capable of survival if the players within it could legitimately resist one another by resorting to the same strategies? Nevertheless, reservations about such a daring and doubly heterodox idea were not long in arriving. They were voiced in a work that enjoyed wide circulation in early modern Catholic Europe, penned by another great Dominican with a particular interest in the world of commerce.

For Tomás de Mercado—author of the famous and often translated *Suma de tratos y contratos* (Manual of Deals and Contracts) published in Seville in 1571, monopoly was still a 'tyrannical vice', so 'infamous' as to be 'an abomination in anyone… and condemned by all sound laws' (Mercado 1587: 48*v*).[10] Monopolists were as much sinners as heretics were and, at the same time, detrimental to the *res publica.* If found guilty, they should be sentenced to indemnify all their illicit gains, and if necessary, stripped of their possessions or even exiled. Naturally, merchants were the prime suspects. Everybody knew that they were given to 'agreeing among themselves, setting the prices of things… with sworn pacts, in a form of association, helping each other in turn, and fixing prices as they pleased' (Mercado 1587: 48*v*-49*r*). But they were not the only culprits.[11] Broadening his view of these sorts of conspiracy, Mercado also looked at those entered into by tradesmen. In his opinion, these too amounted to 'a species of violence… perpetrated by these means on the poor buyers who, since they had no choice but to buy, were forced to pay for the goods on their [the sellers'] terms' (Mercado 1587: 48*v*).[12] Obviously

[10]The Dominican Lopez (1589: 151) also speaks of monopoly in terms of a 'tyrannical force'.

[11]'El uno entre mercaderes, en alguna especie de ropa. El otro, entre officiales, como entre albañies, y cãteros. Si, queriendo hazer una fabrica, alguna obra prolixa, se concertassen entre sí, no hazerla sino por tanto. Tambien si despues de començada desagradasse el official al cabildo, y buscando otro, los cohechasse, que ninguno la hiziesse. A todos estos mãda castigar, como à personas perniciosas en la republica' (Mercado 1587: 48*v*).

[12]Mercado includes among forms of solidarity labelled monopolistic the 'confraternities' (*cofradias* in the original Spanish text), a term which the theologian seems to apply both to trade guilds and to devotional associations. Three years earlier, Jean Bodin had arrived at the same conclusions in his *Response.* As he saw it, one of the principal causes of price rises was traceable to the 'monopolies of merchants, artisans and labourers when they unite to fix the prices of goods or to enhance their daily wage or the price of their work. And because such associations

the same was true in cases where the buyers were the ones hatching the conspiracy.[13] Furthermore—according to Mercado—the murky schemes aimed at subverting the auction process should also be included in the same criminal category.[14] The rationale was essentially the same. It was therefore under no circumstances admissible 'to form agreements with others so that they desist from open competition' (Mercado 1587: 49*v*). In this statement, Mercado was also disputing certain permissive—if not free-for-all—conclusions that had already been drawn and would continue to attract support.

When considering monopolies, theologians and jurists usually focused on how putative agreements might impact the free engagement of buyers and sellers, hence on what was seen as the *natural* configuration of exchange. This did not mean they overlooked the fact that merchants, having reached an agreement, might benefit from their market position, not only vis-à-vis their counterparts in the exchange process, but also in relation to their competitors. They might, say, contrive to bar rival merchants' access to the markets, or simply prevent them from selling their goods. These circumstances pertained to a specific form of monopoly, concerning which a common interpretation came to prevail: if monopolies were a manifestation of despotic violence, and if that violence was what brought monopolists into the ambit of sinfulness and criminality, then merely altering the workings of the competition mechanism,

normally cover themselves with the veil of religion, the Chancellor Poyet wisely advised that we ought to abolish and restrict fraternities'. A little further on, returning to the theme, regarding grain prices in particular, he again insisted on the nefarious effects of the 'monopolies of merchants who corner the market in corn, often buying it before it is ripe, in order to fix the price at their pleasure' (Bodin 1997: 68, 87).

[13]'Lo mesmo se entiende, de los que compran, si se conciertan de no dar mas. Como si llegãdo una flota de estrãgeros, o de naturales aũ puerto, los de la tierra, pusiessen entre se, de no dar por la ropa sino tal precio. Digo si los de tierra, entiendese juntos, o los mas dellos, o los mas principales, que como sean tales, y los mas gruessos y caudalosos, en aquel trato, aunque seã pocos casi son todos como entre quien anda, y juega la mayor parte de la negociacion' (Mercado 1587: 49*r*).

[14]'Lo mesmo se entiende de lo que se pone en almoneda, almoxarifazgos, diezmos, si se confederassen los que pueden averlos de non subir de tantos avẽtos o si uno o dos, o mas rogassen, y sobornassen à otros, que no pujassen, y que desistiessen de arrendamiẽto seria monopolio. Lo mesmo tambien se entiende, en la almonedas mas menudas de casa, cavallos, alhajas, como succede, mil vezes en essas, que cada dia ay de defunctos' (Mercado 1587: 49*r*-49*v*).

and consequently the process of price-setting, might be permissible and morally defensible, as long as violent behaviour was avoided. Besides, there were various modes of persuasion and not all of them were violent—supplication, for instance, was certainly not. Nothing, therefore, prevented a merchant from implementing his monopolistic designs as long as he avoided force or fraud. In such cases, the acquisition of a monopoly position had to be seen in a different light. If this reasoning were sound—and there were many who thought it so[15]—anyone using non-violent means to persuade other merchants to abstain from participation in a sales process would be innocent of any sin or crime. The opposite, of course, would also be the case; if such an outcome were obtained through violence or deception, a monopolist should be required to compensate the injured parties: both buyers, who had been deprived of other options, and other sellers, who had been excluded from negotiations or prevented from taking part in them. Violence and fraud were the decisive factors.

This view found general favour, the most authoritative dissenting voice being again that of Tomás de Mercado. He continued to maintain that anyone who convinced another party to withdraw from taking part in a sale to the highest bidder, thereby interfering with the free operation of the market, committed an offence that was a mortal sin. There could be no doubt about this. Such behaviour plainly tampered with the machinery of competition. After all, what effective difference was there between someone supplicating another to keep down a sale price at auction and the obtaining of the same through a bribe, that is, by an act of corruption? To suppose that non-violent behaviour aimed at manipulating the market was acceptable required a contortion of logic that went beyond the bounds of hypocrisy. It was no accident that, in dealing with this issue, Mercado chose to use the verbs 'supplicate' and 'suborn' side by side, tilting the scales, as it were, from the outset. Essentially, it made no difference whether the complicity of one or more competitors was procured by force, deceit, or some gentler form of persuasion: the result would be the same. The agreed rules of the game would still be broken,

[15]Certainly Molina (1601: disp. 345), Lugo (1652: II, 308), Villalobos (1636: II, 363), Dicastillo (1641: II, 849-850) and Lessio (1606: 271).

and the trust dependent on them undermined. In short, eliminating violence did not resolve anything, still less change it. The market was still exposed to an extraneous dynamic, inimical to its rationale. Moreover, the repercussions were sure to be deleterious given that the immorality derived from the violation of the tacit fiduciary pact binding the players. Monopolies were a form of despotism and could not be otherwise. They came in many guises, and the pursuit and achievement of solidarity between merchants was not the least dangerous of them. Their gravity consisted both in their distortion of free bargaining and in the attendant threat to the moral underpinning of the community as a whole. Buying complicity was in itself an abuse. Subornation was more than just bribery—we will return to this shortly—and in maintaining as much, Mercado anticipated what would be explicitly argued some decades later: the extent to which monopolistic agreements destroyed the political fabric as much as they did the market.

Lastly, Mercado turned to the forms of *monopolium* used by victims who came together to defend themselves against an ongoing monopolistic conspiracy. In doing so, he appraised the conclusions arrived at a few years earlier by Soto.

> Todo esto de los monipodios se entiẽde, si la una de las partes no se vuiere adelãtado y madrugado à se ruyn. Como si los vendientes se confederassen no dar la mercaderia sino de tãto arriba, podriã l os merchantes hazerse à otra de no dar, sino de tãto abaxo. Aũque quando esto se hiziesse, ternian gran culpa, los governadores, sino tomassen a los primeros y los castigassen, como mandan sus leyes. (Mercado 1587: 49*v*)

Now one must perforce take into account that the only route open to victims of monopolists was to conspire in turn, to form countermonopolies. Given that this would be a question of self-defence or resistance provoked by the need to neutralise a pre-existing aggression, anyone called on to arbitrate would do well to consider the circumstances and determine ad hoc appropriate criteria of judgment.

A Doubly Heterodox Idea

Having said that, and while ready to understand the validity of resistance tactics in the face of a wicked tyrannical force, it would be extremely dangerous to think that agreements and forms of solidarity of that nature should be allowed to square off freely with monopolies in the hope that they could cancel each other out. When it came to monopolies, people's main concern was with the manipulation of the markets, but there were also political stakes: maintenance of the networks of trust that underpin society. Although it was broadly accepted that 'political' monopolies—that is, those granted by or on behalf of the crown—were admissible for the *efflagitante* public good (Molina 1601: disp. 345), they were otherwise said to be iniquitous, unjust and deplorable.[16] And when they were characterised as such, reference was always made to the many forms of complicity that perennially threatened economic life and the moral order associated with it. The widespread intolerance of the more 'comprehensive', so to speak, understanding of monopolies is to be found in both theological/juridical and strictly political treatises, whether of Catholic or Reformed provenance. Typical, for example, is the extensive treatment reserved for such abuses by the great Calvinist political theorist Johannes Althusius in his *Politica Methodice Digesta* (Althusius 1614: 671–676). After outlining the political justification for the one allowable exception—monopolies granted by the prince and overseen by a magistracy—Althusius treats at length all the other varieties under the rubric of 'pure tyranny' and dubs them threatening to what the public law ought to guarantee for all, that is, the opportunity to freely pursue the commercial activity of acquiring and disposing of the essentials of life. In listing the commonest types of monopoly Althusius followed the

[16]G. Malynes (1629: 212–213) maintained that there were three sorts of monopoly: *reasonable*, concerning the trade in unnecessary luxuries; *unreasonable*, concerning the trade in essentials, without which it was impossible to live decently; and *indifferent*, concerning the trade in goods (such as spices, sugar, silks) whose use was not absolutely necessary. On the issue of the legitimacy of political monopolies, attitudes remained ambiguous and the criteria for allowing exceptions open to debate: Lugo (1652: II, 308); Lessio (1606: 271); Salon (1608: II, 700, col. 2); Rebello (1608: 638–639), who added that where a political monopoly had become the cause of 'appreciable' harm to the *Respublica*, then the prince or his agents would be guilty of mortal sin if they failed to appropriately reimburse the injured parties.

arguments of two prominent criminal jurists, Menochio and Deciano: tacit agreements to sell above or buy below the going price; stockpiling to create scarcity; manoeuvres aimed at keeping certain elements out of the marketplace by force or fraud; compacts between members of the same guild aimed either at charging more for their work or at restricting access to members of their own families, or simply excluding someone from their client roster. All these activities implied the same offence, but there were also others that had a whiff of monopoly about them: for example, when someone was impeded from 'frequenting a mill other than that of a certain gentleman', or when the citizenry took 'the decision to favour certain factions or parties', or when either the city's nobles or plebeians decided to follow some course of action 'on their own and separately' (Althusius 1614: 675).

Monopolistic practices chiefly concerned the economic sphere of trade, but political implications abounded, insofar as they infected social dynamics. And Althusius does use the word 'whiff' with regard to this last category—*monopolium sapit, quando…*—as if to say that there were certain practices immediately attributable to a specific category and others that 'smelt' as if they belonged there. And it was a much wider category than we might imagine. Althusius implies that the more shadowy the type of manipulation, the more dangerous it might prove. This was why sanctions should not be limited to those imposing their interests on others in an obvious manner. It was essential to focus one's attention on the many mechanisms that more subtly but no less intrusively insinuated themselves into the cracks of society and the markets, threatening *order* and *liberty*. Every instance of exchange, every moment where wealth was engendered and, above all, every forum in which value was attributed to something constituted a vulnerable point.[17]

Notwithstanding certain more intransigent moral and political stances, many Catholic theologians were prepared to allow not only political monopolies, but also private agreements to set up what were in effect monopolies, as long as these did not lead to great divergence

[17]Jacobus Ode (1743: 32–43) devotes an entire part of his treatise to *quasi monopolies*, showing how these forms of collusion are a pathological form that attacks any economic activity, not just trade. Ode was Dutch and Protestant and he taught in Utrecht.

from going market prices.[18] In maintaining this view, they held that, within the parameters of commutative justice, monopolists were not sinners against justice but *only* against charity. Nor was this position that of some lax minority since it was also to be found outside the sphere of Catholic moral treatise production. For instance it was fully adopted by Hugo Grotius, who was largely responsible for importing it into the Protestant world.[19] When tackling the issue in chapter 12 of Book II of *De iure belli ac pacis*, which deals with contracts, the great Dutch jurist began by specifying that monopolies were not inevitably 'contra rationem naturalem' (Grotius 2005: II, 749). Not only was it indisputable that a sovereign might for sound reasons, grant certain individuals the exclusive right to sell certain sorts of things, and set the price thereof, but it was also permissible for private individuals to adopt such practices, as long as they contented themselves with a 'reasonable profit'. Those risking their own resources to acquire and exploit a dominant position in the market were not *ipso facto* to be condemned. Merely having pursued a more aggressive economic strategy than one's competitors did not make someone a monopolist. Obviously, it was not permissible to hatch an agreement to sell one's merchandise only at a price higher than the going one, or to employ force or cunning to prevent others from introducing 'any greater quantity' of certain goods into the marketplace, or indeed to agree 'to buy up all, in order to sell them again, at a rate very exorbitant' (Grotius 2005: II, 750). But Grotius's hard line was considerably softer when it was a question of the arrival of goods from elsewhere and in abundance being blocked by other means, or when a limited agreement might be arrived at to buy up and sell on at a profit, if the latter was not excessive. In these cases, the rights of others were not seriously infringed. Nonetheless, such actions might be considered an offence 'against the Rules of Charity' (Grotius 2005: II, 750). Grotius exhibits the kind of

[18]Theologians and jurists saw these as fluctuating but within certain binding limits, dubbed *latitudines*, or bands. Thus, there was an *infimo* natural price (the lowest possible) and at the opposite end of the scale, a *rigoroso* natural price (the highest possible); somewhere between these there was a *moderato* natural price. One Tomás De Vio, better known as 'Cajetanus' had posited this tripartition. The bibliography on the subject is vast, and I cite here only a recent work by Wim Decock (2013: ch. 7).

[19]On this aspect, I cite here only Brian Tierney (1997: ch. 13).

reasoning that Mercado had so harshly criticised, but it was in line with that of the less intransigent Catholics.

Naturally, some people regarded such leniency with a degree of suspicion, while others—for instance, the Jesuit Juan de Lugo—were prepared to permit sales resulting from conspiratorial agreements if they respected reasonable profit margins, provided that the market was not already contaminated by the monopoly. Underlying the support for such forms of market manipulation was the conviction that it could be opposed and neutralised by those on the receiving end if the latter had recourse to the same weapons (Lugo 1652: II, 308).[20] What afforded a degree of legitimacy to certain questionable strategies was precisely the fact that the conspirators' opponents, whether buyers or sellers, could defend themselves by conspiring in turn to bring the price closer to what seemed justifiable from their point of view (Bañes 1595: 350, col. 2).[21]

This notion of fighting fire with fire found support not only among Jesuits and Dominicans, but also in other quarters.[22] It was embraced, for example, by Martino Bonacina (1632a: II, 402–403) of the Oblates of Saint Ambrose with regard to price-setting between sellers and buyers.[23] Once the monopolist trap had sprung there was really no choice.

[20]'Durante eo monopolio ex parte venditorum, posse emptores è contra conspirare, ne ullus emat nisi pretio medio, vel infimo. Ratio autem est quia persuadere absque vi, & fraude volenti tibi donare, ne tibi donet, non est contra iustitiam nec obligat ad restitutionem; ergo à fortiori persuadere volenti vendere ne tibi vendat, nisi pretio iusto summo non erit contra iustitiam: quòd enim ille iustè potest facere cur non possum ego iuste ei persuadere, dum minae, vel fraudes non interveniant' (Lugo 1652: II, 308).

[21]As the Dominican Domenico Bañes (1595: 350, col. 2) had earlier explained with great clarity: 'Secundus modus monopolij est, quando ipsi negotiatores conveniunt inter se de non vendendis mercibus nisi certo quodam pretio suo beneplacito taxato. Tunc enim omnes isti negotiatores efficiuntur quasi unus venditor, quod redundat in damnum communitatis. Ratio est: quia quando sunt multi venditores non coniurati, facile minuuntur rerum pretia, dum quilibet affectat vendere, quod quidem redundat in bonum communitatis. Similiter etiam peccarent viceversa emptores, quando ad invicem conveniunt, de non emendis mercibus nisi viliori quodam pretio taxato suo arbitratu. Isti tamen poterunt aliquando excusari: si hoc faciant contra monopolium quod fecerunt venditores: tunc enim redimunt suam vexationem, dummodo conveniant emptores in quodam iusto pretio et aequabili, quale posset estimari à viris probis, si nullum esset monopolium'.

[22]Despite the apparent strength of the reasoning, the view often seems to be expressed in rather tentative tones. This is true at least of the Jesuit Juan de Salas (1617: 72).

[23]'Quaeres utrum mercatoribus convenientibus non vendere merces, nisi pretio rigoroso, emptores possint conspirationem inire, ut non emant merces nisi pretio viliori, quod tamen sit iustum. Respondeo, emptores posse conspirare ad depellendum monopolium venditorum, utuntur

Nonetheless, anyone who resisted by forming a counter-monopoly had to be careful: suppose, for example, that sellers ceased their monopolistic behaviour; then buyers, too, would be obliged to desist. Those defending themselves against a conspiracy would themselves end up committing a sin and a crime if—in the absence of ongoing justification—they continued to engage in actions of resistance.[24] All this, needless to say, smacked of wishful thinking, not to say Utopia. The diffidence with regard to fighting fire with fire was obviously not without foundation and it did not go unheard. It was echoed in the misgivings of the Spanish Jesuit and fine jurist, Pedro de Oñate (1654: I, 139–155), who expressed two major concerns. First, if the point of defence or resistance was to redress the balance and to obtain what had been lost, it was improbable that an anti-monopolistic conspiracy would succeed in extracting in full what the monopolists truly owed as restitution for damage done. Second, to imagine that the resisters would not go too far, that they would execute a defence strategy so precisely calibrated as to restore the *aequalitas* of the exchange process, was mere wishful thinking. And these doubts barely scratched the surface of the issue.

This appeal to prudence betrayed evident anxieties. The risk was that the logic of monopoly versus monopoly would transform markets into battlefields with no quarter given, upsetting all residual faith in a mutual respect for the rules of the game. Domingo de Soto himself had earlier underlined the need for circumspect deployment of defensive tactics aimed at opposing the tyrannical imposition of monopolistic regimes. But things had moved on: conspiratorial anti-monopolistic practices had almost come to be seen as a re-stabilising force within a dynamic violated by its own 'natural' logic. In a more or less ambiguous manner, the arguments of the treatise writers tended, on the one hand, to favour legitimate defence—countering force with force when there was no other choice—and, on the other, the right to resist. Naturally, this was not a

enim iure suo, ut se ipsos servent indemnes, & sicut clavus clavo truditur, ita monopolium monopolio depellitur, ut ad aequalitatem veniatur' (Bonacina 1632a: II, 402–403).

[24]'Verum tamen est, emptoribus desistendum esse ab huiusmodi monopolio, statim ac venditores cessarunt à suo, in tantum enim licitum est emptoribus conspirare, in quantum monopolium venditorum perseverat, ut unusquisque se ipsum servet indemnem, quantum fieri potest' (Bonacina 1632a: II, 403).

right to resist such as might be exercised against a tyrannical sovereign. It was more a question of a prerogative ready to be called up and, most importantly, prudently calibrated. In this new economic scenario, the exercise of such a right was understood as a scrupulously disciplined act. It was no longer a matter of plotting or rebelling against an unjust order of things to the point of eliminating its artificer but (only) of neutralising the machinations and rapacious designs of a cabal of merchants or the shady manoeuvres of those trying to pervert the honest conduct of an auction. In this context, resistance primarily meant restoring the delicate balance of forces whose reactive tensions had been upset and on which the equity of the exchange process and dynamics of bargaining depended.

It seemed to some that permissiveness was producing a nascent *laissez-faire*, but anti-monopolistic actions had their moral roots in natural law. This emerges clearly in the writings of another Spanish essayist—and another Dominican—Francisco García. After discoursing on the forms of 'covert or tacit violence' perpetrated by those resorting to 'monopolies, or rather plots' he turns to the one admissible exception, explaining the logic behind it:

> esto seria quando los cõpradores hiziessen concierto de no comprar sino a tanto precio, con tal que fuesse justo, y esto para sorçar a los vendedores, aviendo aquellos hecho entre si monipodio, a que abaxassen en el precio, que por su monipodio se avia demasiadamente subido: en tonces licito seria con un monipodio deshazer otro para llegar a la equidad y justicia del precio, como quando un clavo se saca con otro: pero no seria licito para effecto đ hazer abaxar el precio mas de lo que la equidad y justicia requeria. Ser entonces el monipodio licito se prueva, porque no au cosa tan natural como deshazer una fuerça cõ otra fuerça contraria. (García 1583: I, 378–379)

Contrary to what Hugo Grotius had maintained, monopoly was as 'contra rationem naturalem'[25] and as prejudicial to the free exercise of a

[25] As had been emphasized by three important jurists: Pierre Rebuffi (1668: 385), Tiberio Deciano (1590: II, 139) and Prospero Farinacci (1621: 421).

natural right as it was *natural* to resist a tyrannical force destructive of liberty.

And so it was that, for some thinkers seeking to justify agreements between merchants, it became possible to endorse the formation of counter-monopolies that respected the fair margins dictated by the market. For others, though, such acts remained illicit, from both moral and juridical angles. And if those pacts were always the symptom of despotic ambitions and therefore inadmissible, conspiracies formed to neutralise them inevitably took on every appearance of resistance. It was the writings of the Portuguese Jesuit, Fernando Rebello, that turned the issue on its head in precisely these terms. In the light both of the rights of peoples and that of the laws prohibiting monopolies in the forum of ordinary goods, operators ought to be free to bargain for the best price possible. This led to two conclusions: firstly, any agreement between buyers or sellers restricting each other's bargaining latitude was perforce unjust; secondly, given this, anyone agreeing with others to constitute a monopoly, even within recognised market limits, was committing a crime both against justice and against charity (Rebello 1608: 639).[26] In other words, the permissiveness that regarded monopolistic manoeuvres as part of the natural behaviour of the marketplace was not only hypocritical, it was extremely dangerous for that market's very survival and for the liberty of those operating within it. Yet the fact remained that an agreement aimed at manipulating the market could only be neutralised by a conspiratorial strategy of the same nature.[27]

[26]'Verisimilius tamen videntur in proposito peccare contra iustitiam, quia forum rerum venalium iure gentium, tum etiam per leges prohibentes eiusmodi monopolia, videtur esse liberum ad contrahendum intra latitudinem iusti pretij; non potest ergo non esse iniuriosum praedictum mercatorum pactum, quo istud emptorum ius violatur restringendo pretium ad supremum, atque adeo ad interesse damni dati iuxta arbitrium prudentis obligandi videntur damnum passis' (Rebello 1608: 639).

[27]'Ludovicus Lopez, ubi suprà, post Sotum, & Garciam, quos citat, asserit contra praedictos mercatores in eo eventu fas esse emptoribus similiter conspirare, de non emendo, nisi tanto pretio viliori iusto tamen, ut sicut clavus clavo truditur, sic monopolium monopolio depellatur, ut ad aequalitatem veniatur, quod non displicet, si eo fine fiat, & ubi primum mercatores cessaverint à monopolio, ipsi quoque emptores à suo desistant; alioqui à peccato simili non excusabuntur' (Rebello 1608: 639). The passages Rebello refers to are: Lopez (1593: I, 255–256); Soto (1582: 196); García (1583: 378–379).

Rebello was obviously not alone in thinking that it was not just a question of levelling the playing field, but that monopolies compromised the liberty of the market for basic goods.[28] His intransigent position did not go unheeded and was taken up some three decades later by another Jesuit, the Spanish theologian Ioannis Dicastillo, who argued that even where monopolists respected fair-price margins, their conspiracy was intolerable simply because it was unjust.[29] One had only to look at the markets to see how the interpretations of the more indulgent treatise writers were unsustainable. This was true on two counts: there was a risk that manipulations could make current prices rise well beyond any reasonable measure, and it was obvious that *any* such agreements would interfere with the natural ebb and flow of prices. It was therefore necessary to focus less on curtailing the liberties of those who might participate in negotiations and more on the inevitable paralysis of the exchange dynamic that would result. To suppose that the monopolists would possess the foresight to sustain the vitality of the market, or at least to respect its prior trajectory, required a very large dose of faith in humanity's respect for moral precepts. The hypocrisy of permissive approaches was glaringly obvious. Nonetheless, even for Dicastillo, the hypothesis that, in the face of a monopolistic conspiracy, it was permissible to resist and defend oneself using the same weapons as the conspirators remained

---

[28]Of the same opinion is Esteban Fagundez (1641: 469).

[29]As he notes himself, this view is based on experience: 'Primum propter periculum augmenti pretij ultra supremum commune iustum, quod esset, nisi precessisset talis conventio. Quod periculum semper oritur moraliter loquendo ex ea conventione, cum saepe augmentum pretij in rebus ex ipsa conventione oriatur. Secundo, quia licet talis conventio fiat de pretio supremo in latitudine iusti; excluditur tamen aliud pretium iustum minus, sub quo fieret frequenter venditio. Experientia enim docet, quod, quoties pretium non est lege taxatum; sed habet latitudinem, plures sunt qui, ut plures merces vendant, vendunt medio, aut infimo pretio, idq; sibi utilius reputant' (Dicastillo 1641: II, 849).

morally valid (Dicastillo 1641: II, 849–850).[30] Despite the disadvantages, this was still the only way to ensure that market prices would once again flow freely and that the bargaining process would regain its vitality.

The odd nuance aside, the notion of fighting fire with fire prefigured to a remarkable degree notably heterodox positions that thinkers like Mercado and Oñate regarded with considerable misgivings. And it is true to say that the idea did go hand in glove with two dangerous lines of dissent. It challenged all those who continued to insist on condemning the whole range of such positions as sinful, and as crimes against the *res publica*, and it countered the widespread political intransigence towards economic practices considered so intrinsically dangerous as to demand summary punishment.[31]

Heterodox or no, the idea of *monopolium vs. monopolium* as an existing feature of the market was well enough known, and many of the treatise writers fuelling the debate grounded their arguments in actual experience, sometimes their own.[32] It was on the basis of experience that one could deduce that, if carried through with the same degree of aggression, the defence/resistance mechanism would enable those under attack to fight any violently imposed regime. As Jacques Savary would emphasise, the same forms of association would autonomously and more or less spontaneously intervene in the new dynamics of the exchange process in order to rid it of any extant conspiracy:

---

[30]'Quaret tamen aliquis, an mercatoribus convenientibus in non vendendis mercibus nisi pretio supremo, emptores possint conspirare ut non emant, nisi viliori, quod sit intra latitudinem iusti? Respondet posse; utuntur enim jure suo, ut ea ratione depellant Monopolium venditorum, ut tamquam clavus clavo, monopolium monopolio trudatur, ut utrimq; ad aequalitatem veniatur. [...] Et tamen lege hoc licet, ut eo ipso quod venditores cessent a suo monopolio, teneantur emptores cessare à suo, quo tantum utebantur ad depellendam iniuriam illatam ab alijs, qua non perseverante, neque perseverare debet remedium, eo tantum titulo iustum' (Dicastillo 1641: II, 849–850).

[31]The French situation and the efforts of the police to discover and punish similar conspiracies to manipulate the market and create monopolies are well documented (Jousse 1771: III, 831–833; Guyot 1785: XI, 604–606). On the monopoly as an economic-juridical type of offence, used to indicate many of the speculative practices in *Ancien Régime* societies, I refer to the pages by Alessandro Stanziani (2007: 275–288).

[32]An element highlighted by Joseph A. Schumpeter (2006: 95).

> Mais quand les marchandises sont rares, ceux qui vendent contregagent les acheteurs à leur tour; car les plus puissans marchands sont ensemble des sociétés anonymes, ou inconnues, qui est la troisieme espece, qui ayant accaparé & acheté dans le pays, des autres petits marchands, toutes leurs marchandises pour les porter aux foires & marchés y mettent tel prix qu'ils veulent; & par ce moyen, il faut que ceux qui veulent acheter passent par leurs mains, à moins de s'en retourner sans rien acheter. Ces sortes de Sociétés sont à proprement parler des monopoles qui se sont contre le bien public, & qui renversent l'économie du commerce. J'ay veu autrefois dans des Foires pareilles choses arriver; les Marchands qui éstoient pour vendre, se tenir ferme, & ne la donner de concert qu'a un mesme prix, & ceux qui alloient achetter, n'en vouloient donner qu'un médiocre; de sorte que les premiers jours tout éstoit déconcerté, & tout d'un coup dans le dernier jour les vendeurs, & achettéurs prenoient des resolutions raisonables qui faisoient débiter la marchandise abondamment, & bien souvent les uns & les autres en éstoient les duppes. (Savary 1675: 376)[33]

The key characteristic of the market, then, was not so much the impersonality of the relations that animated it[34] as its supposed self-sufficiency. This may well seem paradoxical, but a natural neutralisation of manoeuvres that threaten the market's functioning or survival, even in the absence of intervention by an external agent or disciplinary authority, seems to anticipate just this. As the moralists saw it, self-sufficiency was dependent on actions every bit as threatening as those from which the market was supposed to be defended. For the dangerous cure to produce the desired effects it must be applied in a circumspect and virtuous manner by players capable of imposing limits on themselves once their objective was reached. It is a surprisingly utopian idea, just as surprising as the amount of power attributed to the economic forum itself and the faith in its capacity for self-regulation.

[33]This impetus bearing on the life of the markets did not escape the keen eye of Jacques Savary (1675: 376); in his view certain *sociétées anonymes* were also forms of monopoly.

[34]As emerges from the analytic literature produced in the English Restoration period, reviewed in an important work by Joyce O. Appleby (1978: chs. 7, 9).

From Moral Theology to Commercial Law

Notwithstanding its radical double heterodoxy, the idea continued to attract support, and it had a second flowering in the context of juridical thought. The principle of resistance in an anti-monopolistic sense was borrowed from the realm of moral and religious treatises and taken up in legal circles. The first signs of this transmigration all date to the seventeenth century. In his well-known *Tractatus de commerciis et cambio*, the celebrated Italian jurist Sigismondo Scaccia[35] declared that, while monopolies as a rule were unlawful and actionable, exception should be made for those organised to combat others (Scaccia 1619: 445–447).[36] The exception was justified, as it had been elsewhere, by the idea of pitting forces equal in strength against one another.[37] Scaccia clarified that in cases where buyers were trapped in a regime imposed by monopolistic sellers, they could agree together not to buy above a certain price, *quasi vim vi repellentes.* This was the same Latin phrase that had been used when the idea was first put forward, and in proclaiming the legitimacy (and morality) of such resistance tactics, Scaccia cited none other than Soto's *De iustitia et iure*, which was, as we have seen, one of the first theorisations of the concept. He referred both to the Dominican theologian's

---

[35]The Roman jurist worked as an auditor at the civil Rota of Genoa. For his working life and its significance in his thought, see Rodolfo Savelli (1987: 39–41). The *Tractatus de commerciis et cambio*, published in Rome (1619), had six successive editions: Cologne (1620): Boetzeri; Frankfurt (1648): Zunner; Venice (1650): Bertanorum; Geneva (1664): Widerhold; Venice (1669): Bertanorum; Cologne (1738): Metternich.

[36]The title given in the summary of the paragraph is telling: 'Monopolium contra monopolium non est illicitum' (Scaccia 1619: 445–447). Scaccia tackles the theme of monopoly in the context of the problems connected with exchange contracts. Bankers too, in fact, were suspected of conspiracies aimed at interfering with the exchange process, and hence the cost of money and associated interest rates: an issue already raised by Salon (1608: II, 593–594) and by Peri (1673: 99–101).

[37]'Extende quarto, ut quemadmodum venditores mercium monopolijs augent pretium mercium, ita è converso (licet non tàm crebrò accidere consuescat) emptores pretia mercium minuunt, & est monopolium etiam iniquum, ut puta, si in portu, cui pretiosissima navis applicuit, illi, qui emere possent, sibi mutuo promitterent, non emere, nisi tanti, aut si in subhastatione alios ego, ne licitarentur, averterem, ut minoris ego emerem, peccatum profectò est, quod ante restitutionem non remitteretur, & hoc est, quod ait Cic. lib. de offic. non licitatorem venditor, nec qui contra se licitetur, emptor apponat: Quando verò venditores monopolium facerent, tunc iustè emptores, quasi vim vi repellentes, possent convenire inter se, ut nullus, nisi certo pretio emeret, Sot.' (Scaccia 1619: 447).

text and to an extract from Cicero, also cited by Soto: a passage of *De Officiis* where Cicero states that is not permissible, in an auction, for the seller to deceive the buyer or for the buyer to suborn someone else to put in a lower offer in an attempt to bring down the price. Soto had referenced Cicero so as to make it clear that monopolies could just as easily involve sellers as buyers. And if the rule of *monopolium vs. monopolium* was valid regardless of who initiated it, both buyers and sellers must be allowed to reaffirm their freedom of choice and their bargaining power through a resistance action that at least threatened recourse to the same fraudulent weapons as those of the monopolists.

Soto's arguments were not the only ones to make their way into the world of strictly juridical treatises. In the third edition of Arnold de Reyger's *Thesaurus juris locupletissimus* (Reyger 1667: II, col. 351), the issue of whether the principle of *monopolium monopolio depellitur* was morally sound is mentioned, and in support of this idea the works of the Jesuits Rebello and Regnault [Reginaldo] are cited. The entire two columns devoted to Monopolium were probably inserted by Ahasver Fritsch, editor of the *Thesaurus*, since the entry does not appear in the previous versions. Indeed, Fritsch had approached the question in considering the ways the justice system might deal with this species of crime (1659: caput XVII, § 31) and he had listed the now familiar sources to back up his hypothesis, citing both the above-mentioned Jesuits and the Dominicans Lopez and Aragon, while in addressing scepticism he had imagined a dialogue with Bonacina. The specific issue 'discussed' by the two was controversial.[38] Without prejudice to the theologian's reasoning, caution was surely called for. Could one trust the circumspection of those who, in the face of tyrannical aggression and having no other choice, had been forced to resort to tactics of the same reprehensible nature? Such strategies required moderation: self-defence called for reacting with equal force and violence, but no more. There was a risk of erring on the side of excessive force and thereby falling into a state of sin.

---

[38]'Verum tamen est, recito verba Bonacinae, emtoribus desistendum esse ab huiusmodi monopolio, statim ac venditores cessarunt à suo, in tantum enim licitum est em(p)toribus conspirare, in quantum monopolium venditorum perseverat, ut unusquisque seipsum servet indemnem, quantum fieri potest. Nos hanc sententiam in medio relinquentes tutius esse credimus, si Magistratus ope huic malo obviam iretur, nec peccandi occasio permitteretur' (Fritsch 1659: Caput XVII, § 31).

The same call for caution is to be found, word for word, in Marquart's [Marquardi] well-known *Tractatus politico-iuridicus de iure mercatorum et commerciorum singulari*.[39] Marquart demonstrated a firm grasp of the important issues. He was familiar with the treatises of the Catholic theologians and those of the jurists, and had also ventured into Protestant literature. He referred both to those, like Fritsch, who had dealt specifically with the question and to lessons derived from criminal law—citing Damhouder, Deciano, and Menochio—as well as those they influenced, including the Calvinist Althusius, who had approached the theme in the more general context of relations between the contractual world and political order (Marquardi 1662: 378). Marquart also took the opportunity to isolate and tackle the same problem identified by Bonacina—whether in the face of a monopolistic conspiracy it was permissible to defend oneself with a counter-monopoly—in order to underscore the caveat put forward by Fritsch: that the grafting of the principle of resistance onto the economic world of the market was a delicate matter.

In considering the context in which the idea of monopoly versus monopoly took shape, we cannot help but wonder at the approval it received. Is it not surprising that, just when mercantile policy was finding expression in rules and regulations that wormed their way into the remotest corners of the economy, leaving very little room for unfettered initiatives by individuals or groups, it was imagined that actions aimed at thwarting such a reprehensible strategy as the manipulation of the market could be arbitrarily embarked upon by the economic actors involved? Perhaps this is where the idea began to take hold that the markets, politicised though they might be and having always been vulnerable to all kinds of irregularity and traversed by conflicting jurisdictions and concentrations of power, could spontaneously set in motion effective self-defence mechanisms. If the natural flow of bargaining and the attendant process of price-setting were able, once violated, to autonomously return to their original functioning, and if this could happen simply as a result of a straightforward reaction on the part of those who, finding themselves on the receiving end of monopolistic manoeuvres, had no choice

[39] For a brief reference on Marquart, see Arthur Weststeijn (2012: 189–190).

but to resist with the same weapons, then it became possible to imagine that markets would be able to survive their own most widespread and disturbing pathology. It was a simple matter of standing back and letting it happen. Nothing else was needed. In the long run, the markets would pull through, regardless of the threat of dark forces lurking in the wings ready to stack the deck.

Defending Commerce, Defending Society

In actual fact, the idea was already splitting off into two trajectories. Even as it gained consensus in the legal sphere, it was being applied to another moral conundrum as a potentially fruitful analogy. The issue was this: was it permissible to resort to one act of subornation in order to neutralise another—as had now been more or less accepted with respect to monopolies?

Monopoly and subornation were to some extent counterparts. If we look back, it was common to juxtapose the two terms, as Mercado had already proposed in his day. Doubts, at this point, lay elsewhere. It was not a question of preserving the rationale of the market and the freedom of those operating within it, but of a new scenario, in which monopolistic conspiracies were seen as manifestations of morally lethal despotic forces. What was at stake was the very survival of society.

Once again, it was Bonacina who initiated the debate. The permissibility of using one monopoly to combat another served him, in a different context, to explain why, conversely, it was *not* permissible to counteract one act of subornation with another. Monopoly and subornation were two criminal practices with much in common, but their putative neutralisation led to different outcomes. The reason lay precisely in the fact that one was the counterpart of the other.

If it was legitimate to thwart—or rather *resist*—a monopoly with another monopoly, according to the principle of *vim vi repellere licet*, the same could not be said of subornation (Bonacina 1632b: I, 579–581).[40]

[40]'Nonò sequitur non esse licitum per subornationem resistere subornationi. […] Dices, licitum est vim vi repellere, & unum monopolium alio monopolio excludere, & eludere ut docui

Resorting to monopoly allowed the victims of a monopolistic conspiracy to put an end to ongoing aggression while limiting the damage of a wicked and criminal action. In the case of subornation, recourse to further subornation would neither eliminate an evil nor put an end to existing harmful and immoral effects. If the subornation to be resisted had been initiated with a view to sabotaging an election process, say, the position would in one way or another be filled by someone elected by suborned—and therefore corrupt—electors. The ill effects would thus persist.

Besides, to suborn was something more than to corrupt. Nor was the electoral process the only one that was vulnerable. Mercado had already applied the term to the manipulation of auction proceedings (Mercado 1587: 49*r-v*). It was typically used to indicate acts of corruption committed in the judicial field: to get a witness to make a false statement or to obtain a desired judgment from a magistrate. Bonacina had applied it to electoral procedures, and behind such subornation often lurked the selling of offices. But more generally, subornation was frequently used to cover any corrupt procurement of complicity, whether a vote or a false testimony.[41] It meant inducing someone to break the implicit oath that

de contractibus; ergo licitum etiam est subornationem alia subornatione tollere. Respondeo negando consequentiam; ratio disparitatis est, tum quia non sunt facienda mala, ut praecaveantur nocumenta. Tum quia in delictis patrandis non est licita compensatio, nec valet similitudo de monopolio, quod alio monopolio depellitur sicut clavus clavo truditur; nam per monopolium factum ad depellendum monopolium non infertur iniuria prioris monopolij auctoribus, infertur verò iniuria rei sacre, dum quis ad depellendam alterius subornationem alia subornatione utitur, tradendo pecuniam pro electione, vel favore ad electionem, quod est intrinsecé malum, et simoniacum' (Bonacina 1632b: I, 581). Bonacina refers to the reasoning made by Francisco Suárez: 'Simili ratione non censeo esse licitum, sed simoniacum, per subornationem subornationi resistere, id est, emendo contrariam subornationem, redimere vexationem, quae per oppositam sit; ut verbi gratia, si sint plures electores, & quidam illorum inducantur precibus, vel muneribus uno oppositore, vel fautoribus suis, ut apud alios electores pro se intercedant, vel ut eosdem vehementibus inducant, & immutent: quia hoc non esset, vexationem redimere, sed electionem emere, & virtute esset emerem rem spiritualem, ut infra de his intercessoribus latius declarabibus. Neque hic habet locum axioma illus: vim vi repellere licet: quia haec non est vis: neque etiam si esset, posset simili modo repelli' (Suárez 1742: I [XII], 521).

[41] 'Caeterum ut ab omnibus huiusmodi subornationis, vitium, seù crimen evitetur quam diligenter, dicitur, quod subornationes, conspiratione, & inimicitiae capitales etiam in exceptis, etiam in causa haeresis testes poenitus a testificando repellunt, & fidem testium omninò repellunt' (Ciazzi 1630: 137).

bound him or her to the community.[42] Its juxtaposition with monopoly suggests to what extent the kind of complicity entered into by monopolists was felt to be destructive of the markets and of the political order as a whole. Bonacina's treatment of the issue created something of a line of thought. His comparison with subornation would become the principal underpinning of the moral complex of ideas legitimising anti-monopolistic action that used the weapons of monopolists in both the theological-moral and legal spheres.

After reminding his readers of what a monopoly was, which of its varieties might be admissible and under what circumstances, of how monopolies were created and of the appropriate penalties for those guilty of the practice, Marco Antonio Savelli [Sabelli][43] also addressed the question of the legitimacy of resistance actions against monopolists (Sabelli 1733: III, 269–270).[44] His point of reference was Giacomo Pignatelli's monumental *Consultationes canonicae*; and, as a result, Savelli also moved away from the teachings of the Spanish theologian Henrique de Villalobos, who legitimised the use of subornation to counteract and neutralise another subornation (Villalobos 1636: 716–717). Pignatelli had pondered to what extent it was legitimate to resort to such behaviour (Pignatelli 1717: X, 75–85), but his conclusions struck Villalobos as unsatisfactory, and for a simple reason. As Francisco Suárez had demonstrated, the logic that it was legitimate to repel a force by force could not also apply to subornation. Indeed, cases of subornation were not comparable to monopolies, which called for a very different approach.[45] Although a monopoly was

[42]On the political implications of the subornation and on the multiple interpretations that derive from its ambiguity, see Daniel Schwartz (2019).

[43]Savelli, like Scaccia, had practical experience in an important magistracy, as auditor of the criminal Rota in Florence. Roman Piotrowski (1933: 206–207, 351–352) notes that both Scaccia and Savelli had looked into the question of the legitimacy of creating a monopoly to counteract another; however he devotes only a few lines to the two jurists, without discussing the theological roots of their arguments or appreciating their full significance.

[44]'Ubi quid sit monopolium & qualiter eius auctores teneantur ad restitutionem, & etiam qui non sunt auctores non possint accipere pro mercibus pretium auctum ex conventione aliorum, an liceat monopolium monopolio dissolvere' (Sabelli 1733: III, 270).

[45]'Nam, et si aliquando liceat adhibere munera, & preces ad aliquid justum, ac honestum obtinendum, non tamen in ordinem ad subornandum. Unde tenendum est nullatenus esse licitum adhibere subornationem contra subornationem. Nam elector subornatus non potest benè eligere cum eligat scundùm mensuram subornationis. Unde qui subornat, quantùm est

a malicious action, like subornation, it was permissible to counteract it with an action of the same sort.[46] By nature abusive, harmful to the community and to its individual members, monopolies also wielded a negative moral force.[47] That is why it was legitimate to defend oneself against them, and setting up a counter-monopoly was an acknowledged way of doing so. Pignatelli felt this was solid ground. A moral force could be confronted and defeated only by another moral force, and monopolistic actions deployed to anti-monopolistic ends were legitimate acts of resistance intended to neutralise dire threats to the community. His reasoning was hardly new, and indeed it was a case of plagiarism since the terms he used were identical to those of the Theatine Zaccaria Pasqualigo, who had in turn taken his cue from Bonacina (Pasqualigo 1641: 230–231).[48] But there was one small difference between the two texts: the substitution of the word 'mortalis' for 'moralis', applied to the force in question, is worthy of our scrutiny. Were monopolies (im)moral forces only, or were they mortal ones as well? We cannot know if 'mortalis' was a printing error, a slip on the author's part, or a happy linguistic intuition. But the aptness of the term used by Pignatelli would not have escaped his contemporaries. Was it possible that the jurist-theologian really did consider monopoly a force with potentially deadly effects?

---

de se, semper ponit causam malae electionis, ac intendit, quod electio sequatur secundum mensuram illis subornationis. Et ideò intendit, quod de se est malum. Numquam autem licet intendere malum, sive in ordinem ad bonum, sive in ordinem ad aliud malum propulsandum. Et absque nova subornationie potest adhiberi remedium priori subornationi, eam detegendo, & manifestando electoribus, ac proponendo motiva justae, ac debitaeelectionis. Neque est eadem ratio de vi. Quia vis, qua altera vis repellitur, non ordinatur ad malum, sed ad id, quod licitum, & honestum est, nempé ad defensionem, vel personae, vel rerum, quae est de iure naturali, & ideò licita, & honesta est contra aliam. At subornatio per se primò ordinatur ad malum, licét possit inde se qui aliquod bonum. Non sunt tamen facienda mala, ut eveniant bona' (Pignatelli 1717: X, 85).

46 'Et pariter diversa ratio de monopolio. Quia monopolium quoque est iniuriosum communitati, & particularibus personis, quae sunt de communitate, ac infert moralem vim; ideòque est licita defensio contra ipsum. Unum autem ex medijs aptis ad defensionem est alterum monopolium contra ipsum; & ideo licet ipsum adhibere, qui vis mortalis, altera vi morali depellitur' (Pignatelli 1717: X, 85).

47 The point that monopoly 'infert moralem vim' was also made by the Jesuit Didaco de Avendaño (1668–1675: V, 229).

48 Pasqualigo, like Suárez, would become a main source of this line of argument, as is apparent for example in Cajetanus F. Verani (1703–1708: I, 239–240).

In any event, the line of theological and juridical reasoning apropos the moral and juridical basis of anti-monopolistic actions undertaken using the monopolists' own weapons had bifurcated. On the one side was a crime on a par with usury; therefore it was debated in the context of commutative justice where the aim was to establish a fair and equal exchange process. On the other was an action evaluated in the same breath as subornation and other immoral forces against which the community might reasonably defend itself in order to survive. And as the arguments about monopolies crossed over from the theological to the juridical, the tone of the anti-monopolists changed. Theologians had envisaged countering monopoly with monopoly in a context where the principle of commutative justice was respected and the resistance agreements in question were limited to addressing price-setting conspiracies. But now, the act of resistance itself began to be painted in very different colours. It was no longer a matter of nullifying the effects that manipulators might have on the natural process of determining a fair price. It was no longer a matter of buyers against sellers—or vice versa—in a struggle to re-establish *aequalitas*. What was now envisaged was an action intended to protect the community from immoral and threatening forces. It is here that the connection between monopolies and the right to resist becomes much clearer.

References

Althusius, J. 1614. *Politica methodicè digesta atque exemplis sacris & profanis illustrata.* Herbornæ Nassoviorum: Corvini.

Appleby, J.O. 1978. *Economic Thought and Ideology in Seventeenth-Century England.* Princeton, NJ: Princeton University Press.

Avendaño (de), D. 1668–1675. *Thesaurus indicus, seu generalis instructor pro regimine conscientiae, in iis quae ad Indias spectant*, 5 vols. Antverpiae: Meursium.

Bañes, D. 1595. *Decisiones de iure & iustitia.* Venetiis: Minima Societate.

Bodin, J. 1997 [1568]. *Response to the Paradoxes of Malestroit*, trans. and ed. H. Tudor and R.W. Dyson. Bristol: University of Durham/Thoemmes Press.

Bonacina, M. 1632a [1619]. *De contractibus.* In M. Bonacina, *Opera omnia,* 3 vols., Tomo II. Antverpiae: Meursium.
Bonacina, M. 1632b [1627]. *De Simonia.* In M. Bonacina, *Opera omnia,* 3 vols., Tomo I. Antverpiae: Meursium.
Botero, G. 1956 [1598]. *The Reason of State,* trans. P.J. Waley and D.P. Waley with an Introduction by D.P. Waley. New Haven, CT: Yale University Press.
Braudel, F. 1982 [1979]. *Civilization and Capitalism, 15th–18th Century,* Vol. II: *The Wheels of Commerce.* London: William Collins Sons & Co.
Ciazzi, A. 1630. *Disceptationes forenses criminales ad reorum defensam.* Maceratae: Bonomi.
Deciano, T. 1590. *Tractatus criminalis,* 2 vols. Venetiis: Zenarios.
Decock, W. 2013. *Theologians and Contract Law.The Moral Transformation of the Ius Commune (ca. 1500–1650).* Leiden and Boston: Martinus Nijhoff.
De Roover, R. 1974a [1951]. Monopoly Theory Prior to Adam Smith: A Revision. In R. De Roover, *Business, Banking and Economic Thought in Late Medieval and Early Modern Europe,* ed. J. Kirshner, 273–305. Chicago and London: University of Chicago Press.
Dicastillo, I. 1641. *De iustitia et iure,* 2 vols. Antverpiae: Trognæsium.
Duret, J. 1583. *Traicté des peines et amendes, tant pour les materies Criminelles que Civiles.* Lyon: Rigaud.
Fagundez, S. 1641. *De iustitia et contractibus.* Lugduni: Anisson et Boissat.
Farinacci, P. 1621. *De immunitate ecclesiarum et confugientibus ad eas.* Romae: ex Typographia Reverendæ Cameræ Apostolicæ.
Force, P. 2003. *Self-Interest Before Adam Smith. A Genealogy of Economic Science.* Cambridge and New York: Cambridge University Press.
Fritsch, A. 1659. *Commentatio synoptica ad nobilissimam legem unicam cod. de monopoliis.* Janae: Sengenwaldi.
García, F. 1583. *Del tratado utilissimo y muy general de todos los contractos, quantos en los negocios humanos se suelen offrecer,* 2 vols. Valencia: Navarro.
Grassis (de), C. 1617. *Tractatus de Effectibus Amicitiae.* Panormi: Maringum.
Grenier, J.-Y. 1996. *L'économie d'Ancien Régime. Un monde de l'échange et de l'incertitude.* Paris: Albin Michel.
Grotius, H. 2005 [1625]. *The Rights of War and Peace,* 3 vols., ed. and with an Introduction by R. Tuck. Indianapolis: Liberty Fund.
Guyot, M. 1785. *Répertoire universel et raisonné de jurisprudence civile, criminelle, canonique et beneficiale,* 28 vols. Paris: Visse.
Hirschman, A.O. 1977. *The Passions and the Interests. Political Arguments for Capitalism Before Its Triumph.* Princeton, NJ: Princeton University Press.

Höffner, J. 1941. *Wirtschaftsethik und Monopole in fünfzehnten und sechzehnten Jahrundert.* Jena: Verlag Gustav Fischer.

Jousse, J. 1771. *Traité de la justice criminelle de France*, 4 vols. Paris: Debure.

Kaplan, S.L. 1982. *The Famine Plot Persuasion in Eighteenth-Century France.* Philadelphia: The American Philosophical Society.

Kaplan, S.L. 1984. *Provisioning Paris. Merchants and Millers in the Grain and Flour Trade During the Eighteenth Century.* Cornell: Cornell University Press.

Langholm, O. 1998. *Legacy of Scholasticism in Economic Thought. Antecedents of Choice and Power.* Cambridge: Cambridge University Press.

Langholm, O. 2006. Monopoly and Market Irregularities in Medieval Economic Thought: Traditions and Texts to A.D. 1500. *Journal of the History of Economic Thought* 28 (4): 395–411.

Lessio, L. 1606. *De iustitia et iure.* Parisijs: Thierry.

Lopez, L. 1589. *Instructorium negotiantium duobus contentum libris.* Salmanticae: Bonardus.

Lopez, L. 1593. *Tractatus de contractibus et negotiationis duobus contenti libri*, 2 vols. Lugduni: Iuntarum.

Lugo (de), I. 1652. *Disputationum de iustitia et iure*, 2 vols. Lugduni: Borde, Arnaud & Rigaud.

Malynes, G. 1629. *Consuetudo, vel Lex Mercatoria.* London: Islip.

Maifreda, G. 2012. *From Oikonomia to Political Economy. Constructing Economic Knowledge from the Renaissance to the Scientific Revolution.* Farnham and Burlington: Ashgate.

Marquardi, J. 1662. *Tractatus politico-iuridicus de iure mercatorum et commerciorum singulari*, 2 vols. Francofurti: Götz.

Mercado (de), T. 1587 [1571]. *Suma de tratos y contratos.* Sevilla: Diaz.

Molina, L. 1601. *Disputationes de contractibus.* Venetiis: Collosino & Baretio.

More, T. 2002 [1516]. *Utopia*, ed. G.M. Logan and R.M. Adams. Cambridge: Cambridge University Press.

Ode, J. 1743. *Disputatio juridica inauguralis de monopoliis.* Traiecti ad Rhenum: van Megen.

Oñate (de), P. 1654. *De contractibus onerosis, tomus tertius*, 2 vols. Romae: Bernabò.

Ó Gráda, C. 2009. *Famine. A Short History.* Princeton, NJ and Oxford: Princeton University Press.

Pasqualigo, Z. 1641. *Decisiones morales.* Verona: Merlum.

Peri, G.D. 1673 [1651]. *I Frutti d'Albaro, overo Il Negotiante, parte terza.* Venetia: Hertz.

Pignatelli, J. 1717 [1668–1697]. *Consultationes canonicae*, 11 vols. Lugduni: De Tournes.
Piotrowski, R. 1933. *Cartels and Trusts. Their Origin and Historical Development from the Economic and Legal Aspects*. London: Allen & Unwin.
Prodi, P. 2009. *Settimo non rubare. Furto e mercato nella storia dell'Occidente*. Bologna: il Mulino.
Rebello, F. 1608. *Opus de obligationibus iustitiae, religionis et caritatis*. Lugduni: Cardon.
Rebuffi, P. 1668 [1550]. *In constitutiones regias commentarius*. Amstelodami: Schipper.
Reginaldo, V. 1616. *Praxis fori poenitentialis ad directionem confessarii*, 3 vols. Lugduni: Cardon.
Reyger (de), A. 1667 [1604]. *Thesaurus juris locupletissimus*, 2 vols. Francofurti and Lipsiae: Felgibeli.
Sabelli, M.A. 1733 [1685]. *Summa diversorum tractatuum*, 8 vols. Parmae: Monti.
Salas (de), I. 1617. *Commentarii in sucundam secundae D. Thome de Contractibus*. Lugduni: Cardon.
Salon, M.B. 1608. *Controversiae de iustitia et iure, atque de contractibus & commercijs humanis, licitis ac illicitis*, 2 vols. Venetiis: Baretio.
Savary, J. 1675. *Le parfait negociant ou instruction generale pour ce qui regarde le commerce*. Paris: Guignard.
Savelli, R. 1987. Between Law and Morals: Interest in the Dispute on Exchanges During the 16th Century. In *The Courts and the Development of Commercial Law*, ed. V. Piergiovanni, 39–102. Berlin: Duncker & Humblot.
Scaccia, S. 1619. *Tractatus de commerciis et cambio*. Romae: Brugiotti.
Schumpeter, J.A. 2006 [1954]. *History of Economic Analysis*. London and New York: Routledge.
Schuster, G.F. 1686. *Dissertatio juridica in Pragmaticam Imp. Rom. German. Sanctionem, de monopoliis*. Gissae Hassorum: Mulleri.
Schwartz, D. 2019. Just Persuasion in Baroque Electoral Ethics. *Ephemerides Theologicae Lovanienses* 95 (4): 595–614.
Soto (de), D. 1582 [1553]. *De iustitia et iure*. Lugduni: Honorato.
Stanziani, A. 2007. Spéculation. In *Dictionnaire historique de l'économie-droit, XVIIIe-XX siècles*, sous la direction de A. Stanziani. Paris: Maison des Sciences de l'Homme/Réseau Euroéen Droit et Société.

Suarez, F. 1742 [1608–1609]. *Opus de virtute et statu religionis*, 4 vols. In F. Suarez, *Opera omnia hactenus edita* [1740–1751], 23 vols. Venetiis: ex typographia Balleoniana.

Tepati, A. 1682. *Compendium decisionum et variarum sententiarum juri canonici civilis et criminalis*, 3 vols. Vratislaviae Silesiorum: Fellgibeli.

Tierney, B. 1997. *The Idea of Natural Rights. Studies on Natural Rights, Natural Law, and Church Law 1150–1625*. Atlanta: Scholars Press.

Turchetti, M. 1999. 'Il faut obéir à Dieu plutôt qu'aux hommes': Aux sources théologiques du droit de résistance au siècle de la Réforme. In *Le droit de résistance, XII*^{e}*–XX*^{e} *siècle*, Textes réunis par J.-C. Zancarini, 71–103. Lyon: École Normale Supérieure.

Verani, C.F. 1703–1708. *Juris canonici universi commentarius paratitlaris*, 5 vols. Monachii: Jaecklini.

Villalobos (de), H. 1636. *Summa de la Theologia Moral y Canonica*, 2 vols. Barcelona: de Cormellas.

Weststeijn, A. 2012. *Commercial Republicanism in the Dutch Golden Age. The Political Thought of Johan & Pieter de la Court*. Leiden and Boston: Brill.

4

Against the Current

Ideas That Refuse to Die

The attacks of Pascal and others cut casuistry to the quick (Jonsen and Toulmin 1988: 231–249; Sampson 1988: 72–118; Ginzburg 2018: 282–300), but it is impossible to say how far this assault also indirectly affected the idea that it was just and legitimate, and perhaps inevitable, to fight and neutralise one monopolistic conspiracy with another of the same kind. Rationality had been brandished in support of this solution. In the first place, both the right to legitimate defence and the natural right of resistance had been called into play; in actual fact it was something else, that was not analogous to either but in effect resembled both and, more importantly, was nourished by both. In the second place, there was a mustering behind the bitter admission that neutralising the force of tyranny—expression of both destructive passion and violent power—required it to be counterbalanced by an equal and opposite force. Despite the flaunted rationality and the call, on one side to the right of defence/resistance and, on the other, to the principle of countervailing power, the argument continued to be doubly heterodox, hence inherently fragile and open to criticism. Moreover, its purpose was to legitimise a mode of human action that bordered both on sin and on

R. Rosolino, *Countervailing Powers*,
https://doi.org/10.1007/978-3-030-37802-8_4

crime, and paving the way to it meant definitively jettisoning the utopian dream that sees men as inevitably perfectible just as their modes of social interaction are inevitably regulable. In the light of all this, allowing the monopolist conspiracies to cancel each other out—as Jacques Savary had observed in the French markets—or, from another angle, allowing the victims to resort in turn to the same weapons as the monopolists—as the theologians and jurists had argued—was not just rash but also undermined the utopian aspiration in its waiver of the possibility of regulation. However reasonable and morally grounded the theory may have been, its political consequences could not be undervalued. The markets would become arenas of ungovernable machinations and conflicts and would ultimately expose order, and the very existence of those appointed to guarantee it, to the perverse designs of dealers and speculators.

Probably for this reason too the idea ended up losing its force of attraction. It apparently disappeared, although it was taken up in the legal sphere and applied in several important treatises on commercial law. The considerations proposed by the casuists continued to be the main benchmarks of legitimisation and reference. This suggests that, if the criticisms generically levelled at the casuist mode of proceeding contributed to weakening the ideological basis of this particular and dangerous solution, then the small corner of the juridical world in which it had found consensus must have been affected or at least not spared.

In any case, we can only hypothesise the effects deriving from the way in which moral theology, as a whole, was fiercely lampooned. Instead, we do actually know about the, fairly circumstantiated, misgivings of various experts within the camp of theological-moral probabilism who—armed with a full knowledge of legal niceties and the intricate world of trade—took pains to express their reservations about this particular solution. In effect, even before the plausible effects of the attacks on this mode of argument, based on rationality but seen by many as inherently hypocritical, its weakness had already been demonstrated by the hesitation of several of those taking part in the discussions on its formulation. Among such testimonies, the words of the Dominican Tomás de Mercado, a shrewd commentator on the sphere of commerce, and those of the able Jesuit jurist Pedro de Oñate, were certain to have been noted. Their warnings had been all too clear. In the best-case scenario, for the mechanism of counterbalancing to function and bring about the desired effects, one would have to trust to the prudence of the man who, after having stopped the conspiracy by using the conspirators' own weapons, would then have the good sense to leave it at that. Trusting in human prudence might even have an element of rationality, but it certainly also implied a fair dose of naivety. In the worst-case scenario, adopting this solution would merely make more room for further malpractice and immoral approaches.

Emerging alongside these motivated misgivings was the intransigence of the Protestant world, and notably the comments of Samuel Pufendorf. In reply to the rhetorical question of whether or not all monopolies were contrary to the law of nature, the German jurist and philosopher pursued the logical argument previously proposed by the Dutch jurist Grotius. Like the latter, Pufendorf absolved the monopolies established by the sovereign, or on his behalf, as well as those emerging spontaneously and naturally from specific circumstances. He focused instead on the private monopolies, activated not only without the involvement of the state, but plotted in secret and hence without the knowledge of the public, for which he displayed profound indignation:

> …the Monopolies of Private Men are spurious and illegal, and do not depend upon Rights and Privileges, but are generally carried on by clandestine Frauds and Combinations: As if some few by a trick should debar others from trading to those Places from whence they have their commodities, or should hinder those that have them from bringing them to market: Or if they should enter into a Combination or buy up all such sort of Commodities, and then stifle them, so that the scarcity may enhance the Price. (Pufendorf 1729: 497)

Pufendorf's words were as far removed from the ambiguities of Grotius' arguments as they were close to the disgust expressed by Althusius towards the same type of practice. It should be remembered that the term 'monopoly' was used to indicate fairly different practices, all of which nevertheless shared the fraudulent intention to manipulate the dynamics in play, the price-fixing mechanism and the definition of the terms of exchange. Whatever form the conspiracies might take, anyone plotting or engaging in them was a cheat and a traitor. It is scarcely surprising, therefore, that the idea of allowing them to cancel each other out met with no interest in the Protestant world.

The monopolists that Pufendorf was referring to, and who had attracted such interest, were those who moved in the shadows aiming to acquire positions of strength. Such positions were not merely the result of abuse but were fraudulent practices stemming from violation of the pact of trust on which the competition mechanism hinged. Both the survival of local marketplaces and the hold on broader circuits of trade depended on this pact. Even the functioning of the simplest sale by auction drew strength from this type of relationship. Recourse to illegal and immoral practices—generically identified as monopolies—had the devastating effect of destroying the social bond and reneging on the shared rules of the game and its very rationale. Consequently, it is not hard to see why the idea of allowing (if not actually assisting) practices of this kind to cancel each other out by reciprocal opposition, or through the mechanism of countervailing forces, prefigured scenarios that were far from edifying.

Obviously, in addition to the need to preserve moral order there was also the issue of protecting political order. Leaving aside the inherent risks of such opposition, trusting in the hope that every monopolist would come up against his enemies/competitors (namely, his victims), who would stop him by using the same weapons, would also mean having to reconsider an important part of the state's role. It would entail drastically downsizing the scope of the state's disciplinary action on the activities and circuits of trade under its regulation and control. This could signify one of two things. Optimistically speaking, it would mean rethinking the relations between the political and economic spheres. Pessimistically speaking, it would mean preparing to witness a dangerous multiplication of cases of a kind hitherto considered deleterious for popular safety. Not incidentally, throughout the *Ancien Régime*, in the majority of European states cases of this kind were subject to the scrutiny of a justice that was anything but blind and always ready to intervene.[1]

[1]The history of the American Revolution offered a case history in which anti-monopolistic resistance—justified by natural law—was formidably enmeshed with state regulation. While

We do not know how much of all this drew wind from the sails of the idea under consideration: whether it was the doubts and misgivings of the theologians belonging to the very circles in which it had emerged and been kept alive; whether it was the criticisms of the enemies who, while not directly opposing it, had attacked casuistry as a procedure; whether it was Protestant intransigence, or, again, simply the resistance of political power. In any case, none of it was enough, and still less was it definitive. The idea did not perish. Surprisingly it didn't perish even when it was dealt a severe blow by the physiocrats who, without attacking it directly, simply pulled the carpet from under its feet.

The Market Heals Itself

The new school of thought saw the economy as a mechanism/organism with its own natural order of life and a space occupied by subjects requiring the most absolute freedom. There was therefore no need to discipline practices that were damaging to the market, since it would be the dynamics of the market itself that would sanction and disempower them.[2] The physiocrats downplayed the problem of monopolist conspiracies to such a degree as to make the veritable river of ink that they had unleashed seem disarming, if not actually pointless. This same conviction dictated the tenor of the criticisms they launched against those who maintained that the free circulation of grain would simply favour the speculators, offering them precious opportunities for profit. Suddenly the thorny

retaining the conviction that commerce ought to remain free, politics nevertheless claimed the necessary right to block those operating in the market with monopolistic aims, debasing both the life of the community and the activity of the market. At the end of May 1779, as a result of rumours that had been going round for several months accusing the monopolisers of malpractice, the Popular Party decided to call a 'general meeting of the citizens of Philadelphia', appointing General Roberdeau to preside over the meeting and introduce 'the business'. There was no law regulating prices in the shops and markets or outlawing such practices, trusting only to 'the virtue and common consent of the community'. As Roberdeau explained, 'I have no doubt but combinations have been formed for raising the prices of goods and provisions, and therefore the community, in their own defence, have a natural right to counteract such combinations, and to set limits to evils which effect themselves' (*The Pennsylvania Packet*: 27 May 1779, Thursday, 2). On this, see Joseph Dorfman (1946: I, 219).

[2]On the genesis of physiocratic thought, see Elizabeth Fox-Genovese (1976), Jean-Claude Perrot (1992), Catherine Larrere (1992), Peter D. Groenewegen (2002b), and Alain Guery (2011).

moral and political question of the manipulations to which the markets were exposed appeared inconsistent, simply because the angle from which it was viewed had changed, albeit radically. What ought now to be the subject of attention was the competitive mechanism; this alone would bind the merchants, neutralising all threats of a monopolistic nature. All that was necessary was to make it work.

So what about men's atavistic and natural tendency to harm each other through actions that were anything but irreprehensible? Turgot, whom Smith had met in Paris during his stays in 1764–6, believed that it was enough simply to deprive such actions of the possibility of being performed and, even more importantly, of the expediency of doing so. In this way, those who attempted to perpetrate them would find neither the means necessary to achieve them nor any utility to be derived from it. For this to happen, the buyers had to be guaranteed the natural liberty to buy and the sellers the natural liberty to sell. Simplistic as this reasoning may seem, considering the events of human history, it was founded on an authentic intellectual revolution based on principles which were presumably scientifically grounded.[3] This is the way Turgot explains how certain illicit practices would be eliminated by freedom and by the fact that they would be of little advantage:

> For if the buyer is always the one who decides whether to buy or not, it is certain that he will select among all the sellers the man who will give him at the best price the merchandise that suits him best. It is no less certain that every seller, it being his chief interest to gain preference over his competitors, will sell in general the best merchandise at the lowest possible price, in order to attract customers. It is not true therefore that a merchant may be interested in deception – unless he has some exclusive privilege. (Turgot 2011b: 107)

Guaranteeing the freedom of buying and selling was the only way to assure the seller of a price that could stimulate his commercial activity and to assure the consumer of finding the best merchandise at the lowest price. Obviously, no one believed that the best of all possible worlds had arrived. Therefore, so as not to appear naive and to reply in advance to the criticisms that were sure to come, Turgot clarified:

[3] On this argument, see Philippe Steiner (2006) and Steven L. Kaplan (2017: chs. VI–VII).

> This is not to say in particular instances we may not find a cheating merchant and a duped consumer; but the cheated consumer will learn by experience and will cease to frequent the cheating merchant, who will fall into discredit and thus will be punished for his fraudulence; and this will never happen very often, because generally men will be enlightened upon their evident self-interest. (Turgot 2011b: 107)

The only alternative to this system founded on, generally guaranteed, natural liberty was a system in which the putative discipline of an invasive state would inevitably cause only damage. There was no doubt about it: persevering with a regulation that was imposed because believed to be necessary and sufficient to protect commercial life from the ever-incumbent deceptions, that really would be naive:

> To expect the government to prevent such fraud from ever occurring would be like wanting to provide cushions for all the children who might fall. To assume it to be possible to prevent successfully, by regulation, all possible malpractices of this kind, is to sacrifices to a chimerical perfection the whole progress of industry; […] It means forgetting that the execution of these regulations is always entrusted to men who may have all the more interest in fraud or in conniving at fraud since the fraud which they might commit would be covered in some way by the seal of public authority and by the confidence which this seal inspires, in the consumers. (Turgot 2011b: 107–108)

If all this was true, the logical consequences had to be drawn. In other words, if state intervention was not required to stop the fraudulent activities since the market was capable of defending itself, then nor was it necessary (or worthwhile) to take the trouble to legitimise actions of counter-monopolistic resistance believing that in this way they would cancel each other out.

Underlying this new way of seeing the problem was the conviction that men prefer, 'or they eventually learn to prefer, to compete by socially undestructive means; on the basis of industry and not of intimidation or influence' (Rothschild 2001: 189). The monopoly embodied both these forms of action—the tricks and the prevarication—but in actual fact concealed a considerable number of practices. Yet both Turgot and Condorcet believed that the extension of commercial relations would pave the way to civilised competition. It would be the trade itself that taught those practising it that it was definitely more useful and advantageous to practice it correctly. In such an open and free system the opportunities for conspiracy, or for the use of political means in an attempt to get round the competition, would not only be fewer but also less attractive. As a result, over time the recourse to illegitimate practices such as violence or fraud would dwindle, and over time individuals would become more inclined to consider and better at estimating 'the uncertainty of success, the dangers to which one is exposed, the reduction of legitimate resources, occasioned by the loss of the confidence of others' (Condorcet 1847–1849a: VI, 527–529).[4]

Apparently, there was even more to it. Seen from this new angle, the expansion of market logic based on correct competition would also eliminate the fear and loathing behind the classic image of the marketplace besieged by speculation and populated by greedy producers, avid merchants and ruthless businessmen. Obviously, the first market in question was that of grain.

As Condorcet explained in his *Réflexions sur le commerce de blés*, decade after decade the fears and prejudices of the people had produced bad laws and, unfortunately, continued to be the main obstacle to a new system founded on liberty (Condorcet 1847–1849c: XI, 197, 200–202).[5] In another of his works addressing the issue of monopoly, *Monopole et monopoleur*, Condorcet specified that this distortion of commercial practice was none other than the result, on the one hand, of bad rules and worse administration and, on the other, of fear and prejudice. It was, evidently, a vicious circle. The poor legislation derived from the fear and the prejudice and, to remedy the irrational instincts that drove the people, the bad administrators mistakenly did nothing but create the conditions for obscure manoeuvres and strategies of a monopolistic character (Condorcet 1847–1849b: XI, 55). In other words, the intrigue was the result of the bad policy itself, which was in turn guided by fear. On the other

[4] I am citing the translation by Emma Rothschild (2001: 244).
[5] On these passages, see Rothschild (2001: 166).

hand, restrictions on the freedom of trade meant that there were few merchants and this rarefaction created the perfect terrain for the fear of intrigue and sometimes for the intrigue itself. The only solution to all this was to liberate the competition mechanism and ensure that it was extended to a large number of people. The way to avoid monopolies was to allow the practice of trade to spread (Condorcet 1847–1849b: XI, 45–46).

It was clear that within this new ideological approach there was no room for the *monopolium vs. monopolium* rationale. After all, if—at least theoretically—the germ capable of contorting any commercial dynamic and infiltrating itself into any activity aimed at producing and circulating wealth had already been got rid of, recourse to such questionable reasoning no longer made sense. In the new scenario, or rather, under the new lenses through which things were now observed, there was no longer any need to resort to regulation. Still less was it necessary (or justifiable) to allow the victims of these dangerous and aberrant monopolistic deviations, to which the markets had always been exposed, to resort in their turn to the same practices. In this way, the risk of ending up in a world populated by giants had also been averted.

Josiah Tucker, on the other hand, despite sharing the political optimism of the physiocratic approach, never lost sight of the significance and ubiquity of the monopolistic threat. In view of this stance, his outlook on things appeared somewhat 'original, independent to the point of eccentricity' (Pocock 1985: 160).[6] Although men were naturally inclined towards benevolence and sociality, they were similarly driven by the passion of self-love, which had negative effects on society. Tucker argued that this passion tended to be mean-spirited and limited in its aims, rendering men unwilling to accept competitors. The fact of the matter was that they would have excluded even their supposed confederates if they could:

> Therefore when you see a Set of Individuals forming Combinations and exclusive Societies, you may observe, that the Members of this exclusive Company are still Rivals, and Competitors among themselves; and

[6]On his economic thought, in addition to the classic Shelton (1981), see Young (1996).

> after having excluded the rest of their Fellow-Subjects, would, in the next Place, exclude each other, if they could. (Tucker 1931: 58)

In other words, the monopolistic/monopolising principle continued to operate uninterruptedly. It spared no one and its strength was incontrollable. Sooner or later, even those who enjoyed its benefits would be threatened. The fact that it tended to impoverish everyone was irrelevant: men had always blindly followed this approach and would continue to do so for as long as they could.[7] Even the competition mechanism was forced to yield to the attacks of the monopolists. And they themselves would eventually be swallowed up by this very rationale: they would not be able to resist the impulse to exclude each other (an idea that was essentially not far from Smith's position).[8]

No one could fail to see that this had a disarming effect. The monopolistic passion succeeded in making economic agents blind even to their own interests. It made men predictable (and hence more easily governed) but, on the downside, it also made the market a chaotic place and, fundamentally, liable to destruction.

Was there a possible escape from all this? If in men this passion was irresistible and prevailed even in the face of their own interests, what had happened to the benevolent social instinct? Clearly it hampered the monopolistic mechanism, but it was so weak that it was totally ineffective in preventing the deriving damage. The face-off between self-love and love of benevolence was a foregone conclusion: 'according to the English Proverb, *Self Knows no Fellow*' (Tucker 1931: 58). For Tucker, the only alternative was to trust to reason—which alone could forestall a practically inevitable expected outcome—to be used as a force capable of stemming the potentially destructive rationale deriving from self-love. This self-interest could not be contained, and still less countered; nevertheless, it could be indulged and directed towards a useful end. There

---

[7]Milton L. Mayers (1983: 18–19) dwells on this important passage in Tucker's work, also noting that he had compared 'monopoly with knavery'.

[8]As Mayers again notes: 'economic man also has a darker side. Tucker sees him driven toward monopoly, and eventually poverty, by the insatiable appetite of self-interest. Smith describes his devious and conspiratorial nature and his corrupting influence on the economic policies of a great nation' (Mayers 1983: 26).

was, moreover, an inherent risk in undermining the vigour of this principle, since it was bound to impoverish society. Therefore, the only possible and necessary aspiration was to give it a direction that would entail complicity in the public interest.[9] This would accomplish the miracle whereby the monopolistic spirit would no longer cause damage to individuals and would allow the entire community to benefit from it. In substance, it was simply a matter of placing this rationale at the service of political action: more specifically, it had to be transformed into public wisdom.

Up to this point, Tucker's reasoning appears fairly close to the enlightened spirit of intellectuals such as Helvetius, but the conclusions he reached were somewhat surprising and, in some respects, disarming:

> Now this politic Direction of the Pursuits of various Individuals to common End, the Study of Philosophers, and the Aim of every wise Legislature, will be found to be nothing more than a strict and scrupulous Observance of Christian Morality. (Tucker 1931: 59)

Enlightenment culture had jettisoned the notion that the passions would lead men to lose control and hence to the destruction of society and its markets, and in this way it had helped to rehabilitate the passions (Hirschman 1977: 27, 64). In harmony with this new thought, Tucker imagined that politics would (and should) also perform the task of controlling and diverting human passions towards the good and wealth of the state, and this included even the more apparently deleterious passions, such as that driving the monopolising principle.

Smith's Disenchanted and Merciless Gaze

Many of the convictions that shaped physiocratic thought were broadly shared by Smith (Groenewegen 2002a, c). Nevertheless, as we know, he was much less confident about the necessity, the expectations and,

[9]Even from these few considerations we can understand why 'the key to Tucker's mind must be found in the unity he effected between the need for economic freedom and that for submission to civil authority' (Pocock 1985: 161).

above all, the outcomes of a virtuous policy that could strip the economy of decades of deplorable legislation. At heart he was also less optimistic about the miraculous effects of a market (yet to come) which some believed capable both of keeping in check malign conspiratorial strategies aimed at overriding the competition and, more generally, of eliminating all violent and/or fraudulent approaches once and for all. On the other hand, it is hard to deny his conviction that 'the competitive regime minimizes those forms of economic oppression that arise from monopoly privilege or conspiracy' (Winch 1978: 97). In any case, for Smith the relation between the public sphere, the sanctioning/prevention of monopolies, the protection of competitive interests and the defence of competition itself was extremely ambiguous and delicate. And, in effect, he made no attempt to render it less complex than it already was: 'Monopoly, besides, is a great enemy to good management, which can never be universally established but in consequence of that free and universal competition which forces everybody to have recourse to it for the sake of self-defence' (Smith 1976, I.xi.b.5: 163–164). Good government would perforce be triggered by free competition, but for this to be established and preserved, everyone had to realise that it was the only weapon they had to defend themselves against both private fraud and violence and potential tyrannical political abuse. This was the lesson of history! (Smith 1976, III.iv: 411–427).[10]

It is well known that Smith had few illusions about the hypothetical possibility of politics becoming so enlightened as to make virtuous use of the instruments at its disposal, first and foremost the law.[11] His notion of politics, shared with his friend Hume, had more to do with legal and constitutional machinery (Winch 1978: 177).[12] It wasn't a question of

[10]Albert O. Hirschman (1977: 100) summarises these pages saying that 'Actually Adam Smith presents at one point the idea that increase in wealth and retrenchment in power go hand in hand, and he does so at greater length and with more relish than any other writer had done up to his time'.

[11]As Duncan Forbes (1966: XXIV) writes: 'The Legislator myth flourished in the eighteenth century, for a number of reasons, and its destruction was perhaps the most original and daring *coup* of the social science of the Scottish Enlightenment'. Donald Winch (1978: 33–35) has also dwelt on this aspect.

[12]'For Smith, in company with Hume, politics is far more a matter of legal and constitutional machinery than of men or any specifically political qualities which they may be called upon to

virtue, and indeed this machinery called for very little civic virtue. Most importantly, it was hard—if not naive—to imagine a policy without considering the interests at play of which the policy was the expression. We could say that, as Smith saw it, politics was besieged by interests to the same extent that competition was besieged by politics:

> The interest of the dealers, however, in any particular branch of trade or manufactures, is always in some respects different from, and even opposite to, that of the publick. To widen the market and to narrow the competition, is always the interest of the dealers. To widen the market may frequently be agreeable enough to the interest of the publick, but to narrow the competition must always be against it, and can serve only to enable the dealers, by raising their profits above what they naturally would be, to levy, for their own benefit, an absurd tax upon the rest of their fellow-citizens. (Smith 1976, I.xi.p.10: 267)[13]

Smith definitely agreed with the criticisms of Turgot and Condorcet, who had attempted to erase the part of the collective imagination that tended to envisage the grain market thronged with the menacing shadows of hoarders and profiteers of all kinds. At the same time, he also shared with both the conviction that liberating the trade of grain was the best way to prevent famines in Europe (Rothschild 2001: 73–76). The grain market had always been dominated by combinations and it still was; it was also the place where the interests of production and distribution clashed most starkly with those of consumption. It was an especially fraught terrain, since conspiratorial strategies were inextricably linked to the spectre of hunger. Everywhere this age-old fear was a constant torment for the populace and a concern to those responsible for ensuring an

display in public settings' (Winch 1978: 177). Emma Rothschild (2001: 233) too has addressed this aspect.

[13]This was the reason why 'The proposal of any new law or regulation of commerce which comes from this order, ought always to be listened to with great precaution, and ought never to be adopted, till after having been long and carefully examined, not only with the most scrupulous, but the most suspicious attention. It comes from an order of men, whose interest is never exactly the same with that of the publick, who have generally an interest to deceive and even to oppress the publick, and who accordingly have, upon many occasions, both deceived and oppressed it' (Smith 1976, I.xi.p.10: 267).

adequate supply of decent-quality bread at an affordable price. For centuries, this supply had been a priority for city and state administrations and its management entailed forestalling both the avaricious schemes of speculators and the mere fear of them that rumour could fan. When shortages did occur, the idea that someone was causing or accentuating them was all too easily confirmed. Political order, after all, also depended on containing such fears and on keeping the spectre of speculation and hunger from people's doors. For Smith, though, this particular expression of the collective imagination—which literature had also fuelled over the years (Ó Gráda 2009: ch. V)—was not borne out by reality.

> Whoever examines, with attention, the history of the dearths and famines which have afflicted any part of Europe, during either the course of the present or that of the two preceding centuries, of several of which we have pretty exact accounts, will find, I believe, that a dearth never has arisen from any combination among the inland dealers in corn, nor from any other cause but a real scarsity, occasioned sometimes, perhaps, and in some particular places, by the waste of war, but in by far the greatest number of cases, by the fault of the seasons; and that a famine has never arisen from any other cause but the violence of government attempting, by improper means, to remedy the inconveniencies of a dearth. (Smith 1976, IV.v.b.5: 526)

Throughout the *Ancien Régime* period, conspiracies were a ready-made explanation for otherwise incomprehensible phenomena. Famine called for a similar explanation, someone had to be responsible for it. There had never been a famine that was not accompanied by the spectre of manoeuvrings by hoarders (engrossers) and monopolists allegedly manipulating the movement of prices by speculating on scarcity. Smith was merciless, even contemptuous, in dismissing these notions. Such bugbears were comparable to those traditionally nurtured about witches.

> The popular fear of engrossing and forestalling may be compared to the popular terrors and suspicions of witchcraft. The unfortunate wretches accused of this latter crime were not more innocent of the misfortunes imputed to them, than those who have been accused of the former. The law which put an end to the prosecutions against witchcraft, which put it

> out of any man's power to gratify his own malice by accusing his neighbour of that imaginary crime, seems effectually to have put an end to those fears and suspicions, by taking away the great cause which encouraged and supported them. The law which should restore entire freedom to the inland trade of corn would probably prove as effectual to put an end to the popular fears of engrossing and forestalling. (Smith 1976, IV.v.b.26: 534)

Surprisingly, Smith uses the same peremptory manner he had used to delineate the inequities suffered by the workers to dismiss one of the most persistent fears of the *Ancien Régime*, and generations of readers have been taken aback by this tone. William Playfair, editor of the eleventh edition of the *Wealth of Nations* published in 1805, made a marginal note on Smith's observations regarding 'the popular fear of engrossing and forestalling… compared to the popular terrors and suspicions of witchcraft', as if the opinion expressed were excessively radical (Smith 1805: II, 318).[14] Where did he get the idea of comparing a natural event to a supernatural one? (Cohn 1895: 550).

Undoubtedly the terror of becoming enmeshed in the obscure manoeuvres of the speculators and ending up in the grip of famine fed on irrational elements that then exploded and became uncontrollable within the collective mindset. Moreover, both legal precedents (Braudel 1982: 412–421) and the stories passed down through oral memory over time had given substance to something of inevitably blurred and spectral contours.

Certainly, the market was subject to all kinds of conspiratorial manoeuvres. The market was a fragile creature: Adam Smith was

[14]'If there is any part in this book in which Mr. Smith has held his own theories too high, and held the opinion of others in too great contempt, it is manifest in this sentence. He compares a very natural to a supernatural occurrence, the possibility a corn dealer mistaking his true interest is put upon a par with that of a miracle. A connection between supernatural beings, and the most ignorant of the human species; for a connection, never supported by one well attested fact; is put in the same rank of improbabilities with a practice, which, even according to the author himself, might take place if the dealer in corn or provisions were to mistake his own interest, and if he should want that superior degree of knowledge and abilities to transact the important business which he is supposed to possess. Would it be any great wonder if such men were to be found deficient in information, or even if they were well informed, if they were still to want good sense that is requisite to turn good information to a wise purpose?' (Smith 1805: II, 318, in note).

emphatic about this. Backdoor agreements represented the most serious threats. Lurking not infrequently behind apparently inexplicable fluctuations in prices were backroom deals and the cabals of profiteers. This was why liberalising the trade in grain, which was not a commodity like any other, could well mean exposing society to murky speculative practices and political disorder. Just such fears had indeed sunk the reforms proposed by the physiocrats, convinced as they were that every market—even that of grain—could achieve self-sufficiency and its own equilibrium. It should be enough, they thought, to allow the competition mechanism to naturally penalise any delinquency contrary to fair play; the miraculous workings of the market would soon make themselves felt (Rothschild 2001: 165–169). In France, even as Smith was writing, the first important attempt to introduce a radically new way of conceiving an economy founded on absolute liberty was going up in smoke. In actual fact, the liberal vision was to find similarly fertile inspiration in another idea that had been circulating in Europe for at least two centuries and that Smith was in the process of applying to the world of work.

The Monopolising Principle

It is nevertheless surprising that after Smith had, with a certain smugness, debunked the popular bugbear of economic conspiracies—namely, the manipulations of the circulation of grain implemented for speculative and monopolistic ends—he then decided to draw the reader's attention to the more general threats to which every market was always exposed. This was the meaning of the passage in which he reminded his readership that the meetings and conversations between persons practising the same trade were almost always the prelude to some form of conspiracy counter to the general interest.

This had been a way of demonstrating a certain distance both from the convictions of the physiocrats and from some of the teachings of his own master. Smith had studied under Francis Hutcheson, who had acquired most of Pufendorf's economic ideas through Gershom

Carmichael (Taylor 1965: 28).[15] However, while Pufendorf had morally censured the monopolist germ in no uncertain terms, it is certainly noteworthy that Hutcheson did not even hint at the problem of monopolies created through secret fraudulent agreements. He stressed the importance of a spirit of benevolence and sociability permeating the economic agents and the market, which would eventually begin to weaken the monopolising principle to the point that it would disappear.

On the same basis, it had begun to be thought for some time that the main enemy of the market was no longer those who stacked the deck or resorted to force, but the state and public intervention. This approach completely disregarded the warnings originating from the theological-juridical culture (both Catholic and Reformed) that had stressed the dangerous effects—in terms of trust and from a political and moral angle—of economic practices implemented through fraud and violence. Since the mid-eighteenth century this effacement had been accompanied by an idea that reached its complete fulfilment in the early decades of the following century: the conviction that society and the market would demonstrate that they could independently organise and defend themselves against these bitter enemies.

But, as Smith saw it, the problem had anything but disappeared. Perhaps there was really no way of resolving it and the most that could be done was to limit its damaging effects.[16] The monopolies were the result of a disastrous and monstrous derailment of the spontaneous order

[15] According to William L. Taylor (1965: 28), 'the inescapable conclusion is that Francis Hutcheson took over almost in whole, from Carmichael, the economic ideas of Pufendorf and, in the course of time, passed them on to Adam Smith'. We know that Smith had a copy of the French version of Pufendorf's work, *De Jure Naturae et Gentium*, translated by J. Barbeyrac (Mizuta 1967: 49).

[16] 'But the mean rapacity, the monopolizing spirit of merchants and manufacturers, who neither are, nor ought to be the rulers of mankind, though it cannot perhaps be corrected, may very easily be prevented from disturbing the tranquillity of any body but themselves' (Smith 1976, IV.iii.c.9: 493).

of things (Rothschild 2001: 64),[17] illustrating the fact that 'natural harmony' was an ambitious goal fuelled by its own ideal tension rather than a reality the general laws of which were to be discovered (Brubaker 2006: 181–187). Indeed, what human society was not exposed to the threatening conspiratorial intentions of a part or faction of it? This is exactly what lay behind every monopoly: a group 'characterized by a willingness to use violence to attain its interests' the benefits of which could only be obtained 'at the expense of a larger group' (Levy and Peart 2009: 337–338).[18] Such attitudes were found everywhere, but tended to proliferate most in the realms of commerce and manufacture. As Smith pointed out, the rural world was less exposed to them by its very nature:

> Farmers and country gentlemen, on the contrary, are generally disposed rather to promote than to obstruct the cultivation and improvement of their neighbours farms and estates. They have no secrets, such as those of the greater part of manufacturers, but are generally rather fond of communicating to their neighbours, and of extending as far as possible any new practice which they have found to be advantageous. [...] Country gentlemen and farmers, dispersed in different parts of the country, cannot so easily combine as merchants and manufacturers, who being collected in towns, and accustomed to that exclusive corporation spirit which prevails in them, naturally endeavour to obtain against all their countrymen, the same exclusive privilege which they generally possess against the inhabitants of their respective towns. (Smith 1976, IV.ii.21: 462)

Despite this, going against the tide, Smith not only emphasised that the problem had anything but disappeared, but also pointed out that, in the emerging industrial society, the new-born labour market had come into being already tainted by the original sin that went by the name of 'combination'. The field in which the monopolist manipulations were

[17]As pointed out by Pierre Rosanvallon (1999: 56), 'Smith pense ainsi l'ordre à partire du désordre et non pas l'ordre à partire de l'ordre comme le physiocrates. Sa représentation de la société est beaucoup plus biologique que physique, il pense en termes d'autorégulation plus qu'en termes de lois mécaniques (da la *Richesse*, il ne parle d'ailleurs jamais de lois naturelles ou de lois économiques)'.

[18]This is the reason why, as Pierre Rosanvallon (1999: 72) notes, 'Il n'est pas exagéré de voir dans le 'monopole', un sorte d'incarnation du mal. C'est en lui que se trouve la source de tous les maux de la société'.

most genuinely visible was no longer the grain market but that of labour. Paradoxically, Smith's reputation had followed an exactly opposite path. By the mid-1790s he was no longer seen as the friend of the poor and the workers, equated with Samuel Whitbread (Rothschild 2001: 61–63), but as the man who had scorned the people's fears about the monopolists' profiteering speculations on grain. These two very judgements expressed by Smith in the same peremptory and radical tone—on the capitalist conspiracies to the detriment of the workers, on one side, and on the irrational popular bugbear regarding the conspiracies of grain producers and merchants, on the other—had exposed his thought to two conflicting readings. But one had then overridden the other.[19] Two decades after the appearance of the first edition of the *Wealth of Nations* it was already hard to recall the moral philosopher who had called attention to the benefit for society of having a high wage level, in terms both of the obvious economic expediency and for reasons of ethical and political justice. It was equally hard to recall that it had been Smith who denounced the obscure manoeuvrings of the capitalists to the detriment of the workers and set the public on its guard against policies that were always inclined to sustain the exploitation strategies of the wealthier classes at the expense of the weaker. While these considerations now appeared considerably faded, the image of Smith that was making headway was increasingly linked to his caustic attitude towards the fear of putative but never discovered hoarders and, to an even greater degree, increasingly referred to his general principles on hunger and famine (Rothschild 2001: ch. 2).

[19]In 1797, not coincidentally, reference was made to the mocking attitude Smith had taken to the fears about practices such as 'forestalling, regrating and engrossing' in the course of a parliamentary debate on a bill intended precisely to outlaw and sanction this type of practice in the 'live cattle' market. The bill was rejected as a result of the vote against cast by Pitt who—citing Smith—commented that it was better 'to leave trade open and unfettered' (Willis 1979: 519–521). On the other hand, as pointed out by Edward P. Thompson (1991: 73), 'the final years of the eighteenth century saw a last desperate effort by the people to reimpose the older moral economy as against the economy of the free market. In this they received some support from old-fashioned J.P.s, who threatened to prosecute forestallers, tightened controls over markets, or issued proclamations against engrossers who bought up growing corn in the fields. [...] There was a scatter of prosecutions for forestalling between 1795 and 1800; in 1800 a number of private prosecuting societies were formed, which offered rewards for convictions'.

The fact remains that, in the new scenario of capitalist society, the possibilistic tone used by Smith in relation to the—apparently forgotten—moral conviction which held it legitimate (because inevitable and necessary) to stand up to a monopolistic conspiracy using the same weapons as the conspirators, had taken on a political connotation. In Smith's words, in the striving for wage negotiation the *monopolium vs. monopolium* rationale had apparently taken on such a connotation, since recognition of the workers' right to resort to the same conspiratorial strategy used by the capitalists had been made over in the light of principles structural to an unquestionably political framework. The four pilasters of this framework were the principle of equality, legitimate defence, the right of resistance and economic freedom (to negotiate the recompense for one's work). There was also another relevant aspect: the rationale had taken on a political connation because the face-off was no longer between generic buyers and sellers, but between two social groups with conflicting interests representing two parts of society (albeit in the course of definition).

Smith's position seems considerably distant from the new physiocratic convictions about what was the most effective and least invasive policy for employing legal despotism and the ambition of knowledge to liberate the minds of the people from the spectre of conspiracies and ensure that competition could yield its best results, even by expelling those who weren't playing fair. Moreover, Smith appeared to newly endorse the old argument posed both by a long theological tradition (first Catholic and then Reformed) and by certain important opinions voiced in legal and political treatises regarding the irradicable pernicious elements that were deeply engrained in the market as an arena of the passions. In sum, it was impossible to pretend that the new economic path that heralded the consolidation of capitalist culture did not appear to be dually under siege. At this point, however, the welding of political scepticism—that Smith and Hume shared—with a pragmatism of enlightened and Whig flavour that enjoined a realistic reading of things appeared to have paved the way to a fresh proposition of the old question. But this time it was posited more clearly and with explicit references to the contemporary situation: could the process for fixing the prices of commodities, and of labour in particular, draw strength from the principle of countervailing forces with monopolistic pretentions? Or, put differently and seen from another angle, could such a process preserve (or rediscover) its reactive capacity even when the negotiating parties appeared like giants?

Although Smith did not openly legitimise the idea,[20] his words projected it into the present with indubitable functionality and marked vitality, effectively giving it a formidable application. Yet despite all that had been done to sustain it, the idea still failed to take hold and was once again eclipsed. This also spelt the end of the notion of *monopolium vs. monopolium* that was at the heart of it. In actual fact, although apparently forgotten, it was first treated with disdain and then openly attacked because considered dangerous.

References

Braudel, F. 1982 [1979]. *Civilization and Capitalism, 15th–18th Century*, Vol. II: *The Wheels of Commerce*. London: William Collins Sons & Co.

Brubaker, L. 2006. Does the 'Wisdom of Nature' Need Help? In *New Voices on Adam Smith*, ed. L. Montes and E. Schlisser, 168–192. London and New York: Routledge.

Cohn, G. 1895. Competition and Combination. *The Economic Journal* 20: 550–562.

Condorcet, J.A.N. 1847–1849a [1795]. *Esquisse d'un tableau historique des progrès de l'esprit humain* (*Fragment de l'Histoire de la Xe époque*). In *Œuvres de Condorcet*, publiées par A. Condorcet O'Connor et F. Arago, 12 vols., vol. 6. Paris: Didot.

Condorcet, J.A.N. 1847–1849b [1775]. *Monopole et monopoleur*. In *Œuvres de Condorcet*, publiées par A. Condorcet O'Connor et F. Arago, 12 vols., vol. 11. Paris: Didot.

Condorcet, J.A.N. 1847–1849c [1776]. *Réflexions sur le commerce de blés*. In *Œuvres de Condorcet*, publiées par A. Condorcet O'Connor et F. Arago, 12 vols., vol. 11. Paris: Didot.

[20] There is no evidence that Adam Smith was familiar with the texts which spread the idea of a legitimate self-defence against a monopolistic conspiracy using the same illegal weapons employed by the conspirators. In the references in his works and in his library there is no trace of writings concerning the circulation of this idea. But, as is well known, many of his sources have remained obscure. Both Joseph A. Schumpeter (2006: 178–180) and Raymond De Roover (1974b) insist on the relationship between Smith and scholastic tradition.

De Roover, R. 1974b [1955]. Scholastic Economics. Survival and Lasting Influence from the Sixteenth Century to Adam Smith. In R. De Roover, *Business, Banking and Economic Thought in Late Medieval and Early Modern Europe*, ed. J. Kirshner, 306–335. Chicago and London: University of Chicago Press.

Dorfman, J. 1946. *The Economic Mind in American Civilization, 1606–1865*, 2 vols. New York: The Viking Press.

Forbes, D. 1966. *Introduction.* In A. Ferguson, *An Essay on the History of Civil Society*, ed. with an Introduction by D. Forbes. Edinburgh: Edinburgh University Press.

Fox-Genovese, E. 1976. *The Origin of Physiocracy. Economic Revolution and Social Order in Eighteenth-Century France.* Ithaca and London: Cornell University Press.

Ginzburg, C. 2018. Casuistry and Irony: Some Reflections on Pascal's Provinciales. In *A Historical Approach to Casuistry. Norms and Exceptions in a Comparative Perspective*, ed. C. Ginzburg and L. Biasiori, 282–300. London: Bloomsbury.

Groenewegen, P.D. 2002a [1983]. Turgot, Beccaria and Smith. In P.D. Groenewegen, *Eighteenth-Century Economics. Turgot, Beccaria and Their Contemporaries*, 3–47. London and New York: Routledge.

Groenewegen, P.D. 2002b [1998]. Boisguilbert and Eighteenth-Century Economics. In P.D. Groenewegen, *Eighteenth-Century Economics. Turgot, Beccaria and Their Contemporaries*, 111–124. London and New York: Routledge.

Groenewegen, P.D. 2002c [1969]. Turgot and Adam Smith. In P.D. Groenewegen, *Eighteenth-century Economics. Turgot, Beccaria and Their Contemporaries*, 363–378. London and New York: Routledge.

Guery, A. 2011. *Introduction. De Montchrestien à Cantillon: de l'économie politique à l'analyse économique.* In *Montchrestien et Cantillon. Le commerce et l'émergence d'une pensée économique*, sous la direction de A. Guery, 7–55. Paris: ENS.

Hirschman, A.O. 1977. *The Passions and the Interests. Political Arguments for Capitalism Before Its Triumph.* Princeton, NJ: Princeton University Press.

Jonsen, A.R., and S. Toulmin. 1988. *The Abuse of Casuistry. A History of Moral Reasoning.* Berkeley, Los Angeles, and London: University of California Press.

Kaplan, S.L. 2017. *Raisonner sur les blés. Essais sur les lumières économique.* Paris: Fayard.

Larrere, C. 1992. *L'invention de l'économie au XVIIIe siècle. Du droit naturel à la physiocratie.* Paris: PUF.

Levy, D.M., and S. Peart. 2009. Adam Smith and the Place of Faction. In *Elgar Companion to Adam Smith*, ed. J.T. Joung, 335–345. Cheltenham: Edward Elgar.

Mayers, M.L. 1983. *The Soul of Modern Economic Man. Ideas of Self-Interest, Thomas Hobbes to Adam Smith*. Chicago and London: University of Chicago Press.

Mizuta, H. 1967. *Adam Smith's Library. A Supplement to Bonar's Catalogue with a Checklist of the Whole Library*. Cambridge: Cambridge University Press.

Ó Gráda, C. 2009. *Famine. A Short History*. Princeton, NJ and Oxford: Princeton University Press.

Perrot, J.-C. 1992. *Une histoire intellectuelle de l'économie politique, XVIIe-XVIIIe siécle*. Paris: EHESS.

Pocock, J.G.A. 1985. Josiah Tucker on Burke, Locke, and Price. A Study in Varieties of Eighteenth-Century Conservatism. In J.G.A. Pocock, *Virtue, Commerce, and History. Essays on Political Thought and History, Chiefly in Eighteenth Century*, 157–191. Cambridge and New York: Cambridge University Press.

Pufendorf, S. 1729 [1672]. *Of the Law of Nature and Nations, Eight Books*. London: Walthoe, Wilkin, Bonwicke, Birt, Ward, Osborne.

Rosanvallon, P. 1999 [1979]. *Le capitalisme utopique. Histoire de l'idée de marché*. Paris: Seuil.

Rothschild, E. 2001. *Economic Sentiments. Adam Smith, Condorcet and the Enlightenment*. London and Cambridge, MA: Harvard University Press.

Sampson, M. 1988. *Laxity and Liberty in Seventeenth-Century English Political Thought*. In *Conscience and Casuistry in Early Modern Europe*, ed. E. Leites, 72–118. Cambridge and Paris: Cambridge University Press/Editions MSH.

Schumpeter, J.A. 2006 [1954]. *History of Economic Analysis*. London and New York: Routledge.

Shelton, G. 1981. *Dean Tucker and Eighteenth-Century Economic and Political Thought*. London: Macmillan.

Smith, A. 1805 [1776]. *An Inquiry into the Nature and Causes of the Wealth of Nations* (The Eleventh Edition; with Notes, Supplementary Chapters, and a Life of Dr. Smith, by William Playfair), 3 vols. London: Cadell and Davies.

Smith, A. 1976 [1776]. *An Inquiry into the Nature and Causes of the Wealth of Nations*, 2 vols., ed. R.H. Campbell and A.S. Skinner. Oxford: Oxford University Press.

Steiner, P. 2006. Le débat sur la liberté du commerce des grains (1750–1775). In *Histoire du libéralisme en Europe*, sous la direction de P. Nemo and J. Petitot, 255–278. Paris: PUF.

Taylor, W.L. 1965. *Francis Hutcheson and David Hume as Predecessors of Adam Smith*. Durham: Duke University Press.

Thompson, E.P. 1991 [1963]. *The Making of the English Working Class*. London: Penguin.

Tucker, J. 1931 [1755]. *The Elements of Commerce and Theory of Taxes* (*A Preliminary Discourse, Setting Forth the natural Disposition, or instinctive Inclination of Mankind Towards Commerce*). In J. Tucker, *A Selection from His Economic and Political Writings*, 55–219. New York: Columbia University Press.

Turgot, A.R.J. 2011b [1759]. In Praise of Gournay. In *The Turgot Collection. Writings, Speeches, and Letters of Anne Robert Jacques Turgot, Baron de Laune*, ed. D. Gordon, 100–127. Auburn: Mises Institute.

Willis, K. 1979. The Role in Parliament of the Economic Ideas of Adam Smith, 1776–1800. *History of Political Economy* 11 (4): 505–544.

Winch, D. 1978. *Adam Smith's Politics. An Essay on Historiographic Revision*. Cambridge: Cambridge University Press.

Young, B.W. 1996. Christianity, Commerce and the Canon: Josiah Tucker and Richard Woodward on Political Economy. *History of European Ideas* 22: 384–400.

5

Who's Afraid of Giants?

Reality Consists of Numbers

Towards the end of the eighteenth century, economic development appeared to have reached such dimensions that human attempts to manipulate it—even concerted actions of a monopolistic kind—would have been ineffective or, in any case, irrelevant. The economic dynamics, determined by the demand and supply of elements considered aggregate, were less subject to influence than had been thought. As a result, the role and impact of certain strategies, even conspiratorial, could be only marginal. What survived of Smith's thought and passed to his disciples was not the conflict between the holders of opposing interests, but rather the conviction that, in a society headed towards the growth of wealth, these oppositions and the deriving tensions would eventually die out. And even if this did not happen, the economic process—conceived with traits and features ever more pervasive and gigantic respectively—would ultimately enfeeble any conspiratorial attempts.

What must have seemed paradoxical, even at the time, was that one of the first attacks on Smith's observations regarding the conspiratorial strategies of the capitalists and the potential legitimacy of the workers' resistance came precisely from one of his disciples. This was Frederick

R. Rosolino, *Countervailing Powers*,
https://doi.org/10.1007/978-3-030-37802-8_5

Morton Eden, the very one who took the pains to write a long book informing the public about the conditions existing in the new world of workers (Eden 1797).[1] Smith had paid ethical and moral attention to the level of wages deriving from the masters' manipulation of the labour market, and to the possibility that defence strategies on the part of the workers could restore its natural equilibrium and even stimulate its own responsiveness. But this concern of his had faded to the point of vanishing, leaving in its place a reading that was possibly more 'economic' and 'closer to the truth', but definitely less political and, ironically, less realistic.

The characteristics of capitalist culture called for consideration of the new dimensions of a world that had changed dramatically in the course of a few decades. Thus the old problem—which was scarcely old considering that there was just one generation between Smith and Eden—had to be seen in a new light:

> Both the numbers of the employers and employed are too great to admit of the possibility, that, in the ordinary cases of hiring and service, either body should combine against the other. No doubt, in those particular trades and situations, in which the injudicious regulations of governments have fortified the employers with the exclusive privileges of monopoly, those, who enter into their service, must, in some degree, submit to the harsh conditions which they may think proper to impose: but this, I conceive, is far from being the case with the general mass of employers and employed in England. (Eden 1797: I, 473–475)

The magnitude of the new numbers ruled out the possibility of employers and workers conspiring against one another: these bodies were too large to imagine them engaged in such a dynamic; or, at least, in what one might call normal cases. Obviously, it stood to reason that in certain specific sectors the government had fostered power relations of an almost monopolistic kind, forcing the workers to submit to the harsh conditions imposed by their employers. But, Eden recalled, these were particular circumstances, quite different from those in which the majority of employers and employees found themselves. Clearly, what made

[1] Which went on to become one of Marx's main sources for part of *Das Kapital*.

the difference in these power relations was the quantity of resources accumulated. Anyone possessing property, and hence reserves, could refuse to accept particularly unfavourable working conditions. But those who had to rely solely on the fruits of their work for survival were obliged to offer it at the conditions imposed by who needed that labour. It was nevertheless rare, Eden continued, despite the unequal distribution of wealth, for workers to find themselves at the mercy of their employers. The means of sustenance for themselves and their families that the workers had to supply were evidently pressing needs, but this was not to say that the employers too were not pressed by other exigencies:

> The ardent thirst, however, for the elegancies and superfluities of life, (which is often the cause, but oftener the consequence, of the accumulation of property,) operates with no less imperious force in obliging the employers to call in the assistance of the employed, than the pressing want of indispensible necessaries does, in obliging the labouring classes of the community to solicit employment from the capitalist. Their respective wants, though of a very different nature, produce a reciprocity of interest. One class wants work; the other, workmen. The employer endeavours to lower, and the workman to raise, the rate of wages. (Eden 1797: I, 476)

The needs of the working classes were different from those of the employers. But what Eden saw as important was that, despite their differences, these needs generated a 'reciprocity of interest'. It was impossible to deny what Smith had emphasised: namely, that the employers needed the workers and sought to pay them as little as possible, whereas the workers needed to work and sought to obtain the highest wages possible. While sparing Smith's observation, the emphasis of Eden's argument was more on the reciprocity of interests than on the conflict, or rather on the reciprocal dependency of their potential satisfaction.

Moreover, the conspiracy was possible when few were involved, and here Eden returns to the significance of magnitude, ignoring what Smith had said about the tacit nature of the conspiracy of the masters. Instead, if one can consider the community as divided into two groups—employers on one side and workers on the other—'it seems impossible that the former should ever be able to enter into any effectual combination in order to reduce the reward of labour below it's proper standard' (Eden 1797: I, 476). Obviously, imagining the community in this way was mere imagery, since no such clear division existed in reality. Not so much because these two categories represented only a part of society, which was much more variegated, but also because in his role of consumer everyone, however poor, was inevitably also an employer for someone else:

> Every ploughman, who wears a pair of yarn hose and clouted shoon, contributes to the support and subsistence of the class which is engaged in the manufacture of these articles; yet he never dreams of associating with his neighbours, in order to compel an hosier to sell his hose, or a shoemaker to sell his shoes, at a reduced price. The insensible progress of society has excited in him a desire, and afforded him the means, of obtaining this comfortable species of cloathing. He consults only his own convenience in purchasing it: others do the same, without calling in the advice of their neighbours; and it is thus that the aggregate demand is formed, which regulates the quantity that will be manufactured. (Eden 1797: I, 477)

Both the division between employers and workers and that between producers and consumers were as reductive and partial as they were misleading. Beyond the weakness of an interpretation that saw the world divided into social groups possessing unique and conflicting interests, Eden's reasoning rested on the major elements within the economic process that determined not only the prices of commodities but also the level of wages. In the face of these, the potential significance of a conspiratorial strategy on the part of the employers could only be marginal, if not insubstantial. At this point, Eden refers to Smith to explain how demand, shortage and supply interact to determine the payment of work:

> Thus, as Adam Smith observes, the demand for country labour is greater at hay-time and harvest than during the rest of the year, and the wages of agricultural labourers rise accordingly. Upon the same principle it is, that, in time of war, when forty or fifty thousand sailors are forced from the merchants' service into his Majesty's navy, the demand for sailors to merchant ships necessarily rises with their scarcity; and the consequence is, that those who are employed in that service are better paid during war, than peace. (Eden 1797: I, 477)

But the reference to Smith's words was an aesthetic flourish rather than substantial since his thought on the matter had effectively been rendered meaningless. In fact, immediately afterwards Eden completes his reasoning by asserting that 'The combination of ship-owners could no more prevent a rise in seamen's wages in time of war, than a combination of the men could prevent a fall in them, when nine tenths of the crews employed in the navy were paid off' (Eden 1797: I, 477–478). As if to say that, if it was not the numbers, it was the circumstances that sometimes made impossible and sometimes vain the conspiracies aimed at manipulating wages. And, given the ineffectiveness and impracticability of any possible influence on the wage levels, recourse to the weapon of combination was futile. It made no difference whether the people in question were masters or workers. It was history then that rendered Eden's conclusions harmless; or at least that is how they appeared for another quarter-century.

Better to Keep Them in Chains

In 1799, nine years after Adam Smith's death, the British Parliament adopted the first general Combination Act. This prohibited contracts and agreements made by workers seeking to obtain an increase in their wages, a reduction or alteration of their hours or times of work or a decrease in the quantity of work. The Act also outlawed agreements preventing any person from employing whomsoever they thought fit, and 'controlling or anyway affecting any person carrying on any manufacture, trade, or business, in the conduct or management thereof' (Orth 1991: 45).[2] The Act also established that 'attending a meeting held for illegal purposes or encouraging others directly or indirectly to attend such a meeting was criminal, as was the payment or collection of money for illegal purposes' (Orth 1991: 46).

[2]In addition, 'one could not directly or indirectly endeavour to prevent a workman from agreeing to work or endeavour to prevail on a workman already hired to leave work; nor could one endeavour to prevent any master from employing whomever he pleased'; moreover, once hired, a workman 'could not refuse to work with any other workman' (Orth 1991: 45–46).

It had all begun with a petition submitted by the master millwrights requesting an act that would be more effective in preventing the (already illegal) combinations of workers employed in this sector and would legislate in the regulation of their wages. When this request of a specific nature was brought before Parliament, it provided the opportunity for establishing a more general principle. The idea was the brainchild of the evangelical MP William Wilberforce,[3] who not only declared himself in favour of the bill but also invited his colleagues to discuss the expediency of extending the measure to all workers, establishing a general rather than particular disciplinary criterion. After all, Wilberforce observed, the combinations were a widespread evil that was hard to circumscribe, so that it would be opportune to pass legislation that comprised all forms of combination, irrespective of sector. This would mean addressing the present circumstance and also preventing a future reappearance of the phenomenon in other productive and commercial sectors, and would save Parliament having to address a succession of different appeals and disputes on the same matter.

Almost eighty years had passed since Parliament had intervened to discipline the workers employed in the tailoring trade, forced to resort to a strike to negotiate better wage conditions. The ensuing debate led to the implementation of the first Combination Act (1721), and to 'an early prosecution of journeymen for criminal conspiracy' (Orth 1991: 6). In 1726, it had been the weavers, 'covering the venerable woollen trade throughout the country', then in 1749 and again in 1777 the hatters, and in 1796 the workers employed in 'the paper-making industry' (Orth 1991: 11, 15, 18–19). Finally, in 1799, the umpteenth dispute provided the opportunity to transform the rule that had been applied each time to a particular case into a general regulation. The Prime Minister, William Pitt, immediately grasped this opportunity. In addition to extending the ban on combination, that is conspiracy, to all workers regardless of the sector they were employed in, the 1799 legislation also established a summary procedure for offenders in place of the normal common law trial (Orth 1991: ch. 3).

[3] *Parliamentary Register*, 8 (1799): 323. Wilberforce was by this time already known as one of the leading exponents of the movement for the abolition of slavery.

And what about Smith? His reputation had definitely undergone review and conflicting uses of his ideas had begun to circulate (Rothschild 2001: ch. 2). Despite the ambiguity of his warnings about the conflict of interest between workers and masters, and the use by the latter of strategies that could be seen as questionable, in many respects these observations still seemed to go against the grain. Those who had read his words would clearly have needed a fair dose of hypocrisy to believe that combinations were the germs of a disease that had infiltrated certain sectors of the world of work and were now threatening the harmony and solidity of society as a whole. Indeed, the few who had opposed approval of the bill found the fundamental elements to support their arguments in Smith's words (Willis 1979: 516).

Sir Francis Burdett made references to Smith that were somewhat ambiguous, if not paradoxical, and did not truly espouse his thought.[4] As Burdett saw it, the intention of the measure under discussion was arguably excessive and indubitably superfluous, since the—just and reasonable—objective that the drafters of the bill wished to pursue could be adequately achieved by existing legislation. That said, Burdett 'believed that there was seldom a combination of the kind complained of, without a great grievance to provoke it'.[5] As if to say that things ought to be considered with greater honesty, and if this was done it would inevitably emerge that many of the combinations under discussion were the result of something else that had not been taken into due consideration. Smith's shadow was evident and pertinent. But above all, and here Burdett made explicit reference to what was written in the *Wealth of Nations*: the wise policy of every well-regulated state was 'to leave trade of every kind to find its own level'.[6] The labour market was no exception.

Burdett's friend, Benjamin Hobhouse,[7] then added that the proposed measure amounted to legislative interference in price regulation, in this

[4] *Parliamentary Register*, 8 (1799): 687.
[5] *Parliamentary Register*, 8 (1799): 687.
[6] *Parliamentary Register*, 8 (1799): 687.
[7] *Parliamentary Register*, 9 (1799): 65.

case that of labour, which might nonetheless be seen as property. Allowing Parliament to intervene in these terms with a general measure regarding all sectors depending on the buying and selling of labour was tantamount to exposing a natural right to political authority. Most importantly, it could not be denied that combinations among workers were easier to quash than those among masters. They were weaker and hence less dangerous, since the resources of the workers were destined to run out rapidly, unlike those of the masters. Therefore they had an extremely limited capacity to resist. It was abundantly clear that very shortly after launching their protest they would find themselves constrained to abandon it and accept re-employment at the old contractual conditions. Clearly, therefore, the principle underlying the bill in question could scarcely be defended. In substance, this argument was an evident reference to the thoughts of Smith, although Hobhouse chose not to cite him explicitly.

Moreover, as Lord Holland pointed out,[8] taking such action entailed the risk of provoking an effect contrary to the intentions of those who had proposed the bill. Legislation against workers' conspiracies already existed and was widely applied. Furthermore, every time that politics had intervened in the wage-fixing process it had had a different effect on the two parties involved. The interests were conflicting but the terms were not equal. This inequality—and it was here that Smith's ideas returned to the fore—was ever greater and increasingly in favour of the masters. Therefore consideration had to be given to the fact that the extension of the prohibition, hitherto applied to individual sectors, to a general law to be applied to every kind of combination regardless of the type of workers involved, would further weaken the already weaker party. Moreover, Holland went on, no one was taking into consideration what Smith had emphasised twenty-five years earlier: namely, the inclination of the masters to conspire against the workers, both tacitly and in the form of explicit agreements. Holland went on to read several passages from the *Wealth of Nations* for those who were not familiar with it.[9] Already in Smith's time, when the legislation and the judges' attitudes were less

[8] *Parliamentary Register*, 9 (1799): 562–565.

[9] *Parliamentary Register*, 9 (1799): 563.

harsh than they had recently become, the inequality of treatment led to enormous consequences. It was therefore not hard to imagine what would happen if such a bill were approved. Politics could not tarnish itself with the infamy of further prejudicing the rest of the world against the lower and less fortunate classes. The masters had always sought to accuse their workers of conspiratorial attitudes and designs, which were understandably always aimed at raising their wages. This followed logically as a matter of course. However, it would be politically inappropriate to enchain such logic or, still worse, to enforce complete immobility. It was similarly inappropriate to prejudice *a priori* any alterations to these relations of power. No one could know what history had in store.

> It must be evident to their Lordships, that circumstances might arise which might render an increase of workmen's wages necessary, on principles of justice and humanity; but if such a bill as this should be suffered to pass, no fair attempt could ever be made on the part of the journeymen to get their wages increased, without subjecting them to the pains and penalties of this act (Holland).[10]

If there were a possibility that wages should not remain anchored to the low levels that only just allowed the workers to survive on them, then this possibility depended on the workers being able to resort to the same weapon widely used by their masters. For over a century, theorists and jurists had taught that a monopolist conspiracy could only be countered by another of the same kind. After its long circulation, this idea seemed to have been completely mislaid. But, in the wake of Smith's words, it was actually still alive.

Now, in 1799, prohibiting combinations among workers meant not only freezing wage levels and definitively depriving them of flexibility, but also separating them completely from all the other components of the economic process. In this way, if the circumstances had made an increase in the price of work just and expedient—and not only for ethical-political reasons—no attempt in such a direction would have met with success since no one would be in a condition to sustain and defend

[10] *Parliamentary Register*, 9 (1799): 564.

it. The tension in Holland's words was palpable; it was a reminder that Smith had not been entirely forgotten and the reappraisal of his repute had not yet been entirely accomplished.

As Edward P. Thompson (1991: 550–551) observed, the Combination Acts were 'passed by a Parliament of anti-Jacobins and landowners, whose first concern was to add to the existing legislation intimidating political reformers'. In effect, the fear of political violence caused by the recent memories of the Reign of Terror in France probably had an important role (Dicey 1904: 518–519).[11] But it was not only that. English public opinion was nourished both by the fear of conspiracies—partly due to what Europe knew of Jacobin policy—and by the tradition of a paternalistic government that was very congenial to the Tory policy of the time. This traditional culture had two salient features. The first related to the notion that the workers had the duty to work for a reasonable wage, or one that was customarily recognised as such. The second related to the state's duty to guarantee a minimum for the subsistence of the workers who were unable to find work and for those who did not earn enough. As has been emphasised by Albert V. Dicey, the Speenhamland system (recognition of the 'right to live', as endorsed by the magistrates of Berkshire) and the Combination Act had the same ideological matrix (Dicey 2008: 73).[12]

But it would be misleading, if not erroneous, to read the events in England 'as a reflected glow from the storming of the Bastille' (Thompson 1991: 111). Thompson emphasises that the agitation of the 1790s was extremely intensive and far-reaching, even though it lasted only a few short years from 1792 to 1796.[13] At this time in the mid-1790s the world of labour was in turmoil; and it was not only the workers employed

[11]George M. Trevelyan (1922: 200) also considered these laws as 'a relic of the days of anti-Jacobin panic'.

[12]The decision taken at a meeting held in Speenhamland, in Berkshire, on 6 May 1795 established that the State would top up workers' wages with a subsidy calculated on a sliding scale and linked to the price of bread, in order to ensure a minimum income for the poor irrespective of their wages. On the ideology that led to the adoption of this measure, on the effects and the movement that led to its suppression, see the still fundamental pages of Karl Polanyi (1944: ch. 7).

[13]'It altered the subpolitical attitudes of the people, affected class alignments, and initiated traditions which stretch forward into the present century' (Thompson 1991: 111).

in the recently industrialised sectors of production who were claiming their rights and, more generally, making their threatening claims heard. Although these claims were stifled at birth, they nevertheless played a decisive role in moulding the consciousness of the workers (Thompson 1991: 113–114, 194).

The perverse effects of the attitude assumed by the State through the approval of the Combination Act of 1799 very soon became evident. Different social worlds, such as that of the Jacobins and that of the 'illegal unions', not only had the chance to mature and ferment, but were actually pushed into one another's arms. The Trade Unions went underground, occupying a secret dimension hostile to public powers, and soon found themselves within a movement of a general character (Webb and Webb 1911: ch. II).[14] But in actual fact, even before Parliament had approved the 'odious legislation', the factories had begun to generate social energies that were undermining 'the very course of Nature' (Thompson 1991: 207). More specifically, the cotton mill had become the symbol of what was perceived in some quarters as the outcome of an unforeseen parturition. The workers on one hand, and the owners of new industrial wealth on the other, constituted concrete threats to the survival of a crumbling order. More than anything, political scenarios with disturbing gigantic presences loomed on the horizon. In this situation, the words of John Thelwall must have sounded as threatening then as they are formidable to us now:

> The fact is, that Monopoly, and the hideous accumulation of capital in a few hands, like all diseases not absolutely mortal, carry, in their own enormity, the seeds of cure. Man is, by is very nature, social and communicative—proud to display the little knowledge he possesses, and eager, as opportunity presents, to increase his store. Whatever presses men together, therefore, though it may generate some vices, is favourable to the diffusion of knowledge, and ultimately promotive of human liberty.

[14]Nevertheless, Thompson (1991: 550–552) maintains that the Combination Laws did not make illegal realities that had been hitherto legal: 'There was, in fact, sufficient legislation before the 1790s to make almost any conceivable trade union activity liable to prosecution – as conspiracies in common law, for breach the contract, for leaving work unfinished, or under Statute law covering separate industries' (Thompson 1991: 550).

> Hence every large workshop and manufactory is a sort of political society, which no act of Parliament can silence, and no magistrate disperse. (Thelwall 1796: 21)

Thelwall was referring to the two famous Acts promulgated by Parliament in 1795 and known as the *Gagging Acts* (Hampsher-Monk 1991: 5).[15] But there was much more to this short passage in his *Letter*. By bringing together the effects of the economic transformations on men—and not just in terms of socialisation—with the natural spontaneity of actions of resistance, he appeared to have evoked what John Millar had already pointed out. In short, that in commercial societies, in which men were naturally inclined to socialise, there was a greater propensity to react in the event of a tyrannical threat. Millar had emphasised the fact that commerce made societies less prone to abuses and violence since they featured a spontaneous readiness to resist. This resistance assumed that men talked to each other, and this interchange was stimulated by commerce which depended on negotiation. Thelwall, however, was not thinking of commerce, since what he had before his eyes was the new industrial world of the factories.[16] In this world, men's dealings with each other were spurred by the interests to be pursued and/or the needs to be satisfied. This was a form of exchange too, but the motivations behind it were quite different from those of the people engaged in commercial activities. The aspect that is most pertinent to the topic being dealt with here is that Thelwall, with his somewhat visionary and prophetic gaze, had unwittingly recolled the very idea that had previously led to the concept of *monopolium vs monopolium*. This appeared to have been mislaid along the way, but instead it was still there, alive and kicking and making its strength felt, and now—to an even greater degree—its striking functionality within the contemporary scene.

---

[15]That wasn't all. Behind the ban to resort to the weapon of combination for many workmen (this was actually tolerated for 'factors, merchants, wholesale dealers and opulent manufacturers')—then definitively endorsed in the act of 1799—there was another issue related to the lack of representation, in turn linked to a difference in treatment, and hence to a question of inequality (Hampsher-Monk 1991: 5).

[16]Thelwall referred in his writings to both Locke and Smith to maintain that an economy such as the one which was taking shape denied the workers both their original rights to the land and a just recompense for their labour (Hampsher-Monk 2006: 685).

Thelwall's warning was clear. How was it possible not to realise that the accumulation of capital in just a few hands would reinstate the tyrannical threat of monopoly?[17] At the same time, Thelwall also realised that this threat—in many respects similar to a disease—brought with it, or naturally produced, the antibodies for its own treatment.[18] The old principle, whereby any monopolist dynamic could only (and rightly) be offset by a counter-monopolist dynamic, had been restyled in political terms in the new context of the class struggle.

By extending the prohibition on association to all workers and endorsing a general criterion, the Combination Act of 1799 had codified 'existing anti-trade union law, simplifying the procedure, and enabling two magistrates to proceed by summary jurisdiction' (Thompson 1991: 551).[19] Moreover, as Thompson reminds us, the new rules never entirely replaced the old legislation which acknowledged the magistrates' prerogative 'to arbitrate in wage disputes' (Thompson 1991: 551–552).[20] Indeed, it was not rare for legal disputes to refer to the common law which had hitherto been used to sanction the conspiratorial actions of the workers. Despite this, the changes were evident, and more specifically it was evident how prejudicial the Act of 1799 was towards any attempts at manoeuvre made by journeymen and workmen in the cramped space of wage negotiation. Not surprisingly, actions of resistance did take shape and Parliament was flooded with petitions from all over the country (Orth 1991: 49).[21] The response was almost immediate. At this point,

[17]The bargaining between employers and workers to define wages concealed a form of 'monopolistic extortion', which patently involved the negation of certain principles of natural law; the workers were obliged to deal with subjects that were not acting in the market as individuals, but were, in effect, members of a 'corporation' (Hampsher-Monk 1991: 17).

[18]'Consequently Thelwall did not attempt to revive a 'moral economy' of just prices and fair wages either, since wages were to be proportionate to profit, not to the cost of living. Instead he proposed a new vision of economic justice centering on the contractual relations between worker and employer' (Caeys 1994: 274).

[19]The elements of continuity had already been noted by M. Dorothy George (1936: 172–178).

[20]'Thus it was that prosecutions often took place, not under the Acts of 1799-1800, but under previous legislation – the common law of conspiracy, or under the Elizabethan Statute of Artificers (5 Eliz. c. 4) penalizing workers for leaving works unfinished' (Thompson 1991: 553).

[21]'The Combination Act was criticised for vagueness; the specific offences of endeavouring to prevail on a workman to leave and of refusing to work with a particular workman were singled out. These, of course struck at the source of workmen's power, control over the supply of

the intention of generalising a principle that could no longer hold only for certain specific categories, but had to be valid for anyone working in industrial and commercial activities, was further driven home. One year later, the British Parliament replaced the Combination Act of 1799 with a new act, clarifying the definition of an illegal agreement. In essence, the ban was extended to capitalists. From then on, all the contracts made by employers 'for reducing the wages of workmen, or for adding to or altering the usual hours or time of working, or for increasing the quantity of work' also became illegal; thus, Parliament 'outlawed collective action and voided collective agreements' (Orth 1991: 51, 55). Any negotiation had to be done by individuals not groups. The very existence of a group, as indeed it always had, foreshadowed a conspiratorial action that was by its nature a threat to the maintenance of order. At this point, the function of the judicial prerogative underwent a significant modification, because—as has been pointed out—'within the new legislative scheme the role of the justice of the peace was to prevent group action and to enforce the individual contract, eked out by the law of master and servant. In place of their historic role as regulators they received a limited role as arbitrators' (Orth 1991: 55).

The almost definitive withdrawal of the state from the sphere of wage regulation had been sealed by the urgency of imposing a negotiation limited to the one-to-one. Was this the triumph of the world envisaged by Smith? Can we or should we be surprised that no objection was raised in Parliament by those who had opposed the passing of the 1799 bill by calling up Smith's ideas?[22]

If truth be told, it was not just the opponents of the 1799 bill that remained silent: there was no opposition of any kind. Therefore, we have to ask ourselves whether the absence of debate and the (presumably) broad consensus indicated that the Parliamentary action coincided completely with the dominant public opinion of the time. At the end of

labour. But none of the petitions made extensive criticism of the substantive sections, and none protested at the absence of wage regulation. It was the procedures that attracted most attention' (Orth 1991: 49).

[22]As has been noted by Willis (1979: 516), 'Many of those who invoked the authority of Adam Smith in opposing the 1799 Combination Act made no objection to the 1800 act'. On the ways of using (and misunderstanding) Smith's view during the debate on Combination Laws, see Eli Ginzberg (2002: 175–196).

the day, the Combination Acts, apparently (and actually, at the beginning) aimed at the world of labour, revealed a Parliament determined to outlaw every form of combination (Dicey 2008: 69–72). There can be no doubt about the fact that these two Acts, the second passed just one year after the first, were clearly intended to counter and prevent conspiracies of any kind. This was exactly what 'combination' meant.

The hypothesis to which Smith had ambiguously paved the way—namely to acknowledge the workers' right to use the weapon of combination in their turn as a form of resistance—appeared clearly dangerous and inopportune, not to all the English but certainly to the part represented in Parliament. Nevertheless, Smith was given credit for one thing. His observations had evidently hit the mark, as witnessed by the replacement of the 1799 Combination Act with that approved the following year. The germs of the feared disease that emerged with the dangerous signs of conspiracy had not only contaminated the world of work. The masters were as tainted with it as the wage earners, and their strategies were as harmful to society as those of the workers. But not everyone saw it that way. Some believed that the interpretation that had led to the new political direction was deeply mistaken. Driven possibly by the protests of the workers, or perhaps influenced by the now-famous passage from the *Wealth of Nations*, Parliament had let itself be duped by convictions that were anything but real. This point of view was expressed by George Phillips during the debate on the Apprentice Law:

> Adam Smith thought that combinations among workmen were not dangerous—because they were counteracted by combinations among the master manufacturers, which he believed to be more frequent. That able writer was mistaken in the fact and his reasoning was consequently erroneous. Masters, it was true, might have a common interest in reducing the rate of wages—but the opposition among them was so much greater and more powerful than that among the workmen, that it prevented them from frequently combining together. On the other hand, the journeymen

> drove the reluctant into combination, through terror—and the apprehensive, by the hope of protection and security which their great numbers held out.[23]

This was in 1814, over a decade since the passing of the Combination Acts, but evidently the issue was anything but closed.[24] What must have surprised Smith's readers was the way in which his thought had been distorted. He had not said that the combinations of the workers were less dangerous because they were offset by those of the masters. If anything, he had said that they were actionable and were indeed frequently the subject of legal proceedings. He had also said that they were less effective than those of the masters because the workers did not have sufficient strength to maintain their position. This was why their actions of resistance often proved vain. Finally, he had further said that every time the workers attempted to implement such strategies they came up against the harshest social disapproval.

Phillips had indeed gone further, criticising the way in which Smith, on the one hand, considered the strength of the conspiracies of the masters and, on the other hand, the feebleness of those attempted by the workers. The combinations between masters—which for Smith when they were not explicit were tacit—were for Phillips an entirely marginal phenomenon. Where Smith had seen in these a fundamental complicity, Phillips discerned a marked tension if not actual conflict. It was true that the masters were bound by a common interest in keeping wage levels low, but the force of competition was such as to prevent them acting together in solidarity. Conversely, opposition among the workers was not so decisive, or in any case it was not strong enough to prevent them from pursuing the common interest in keeping the wage level as high as possible. Even those workers who were reluctant to take part in the combinations were induced to do so, either by the overbearing attitudes of those who were convinced of the validity of the struggle or by the promises of

---

[23] *Parliamentary Debates*, 27 (1813–1814): coll. 572–573. On this passage, see Rothschild (2001: 93).

[24] As argued by Moher (1988: 90): 'Despite the vigorous opposition of the organised journeymen, Parliament had swept away in 1813-14 most of the old legislation regulating wages and apprenticeship'.

protection and security offered. Therefore, while the combinations of the masters were, at the end of the day, of marginal impact, those between workers were by now an alarmingly widespread phenomenon.

The Economic Rebirth of a Moral Principle

In the same year of 1814 when Phillips spoke in Parliament, mystifying the thought of Smith, Francis Place decided to exert himself for the repeal of the Combination Acts. At the beginning, on his own admission, he appeared to make little progress in this direction, despite having been engaged with the nefarious effects of these odious laws for some time (Wallas 1898: 203). In 1811, in the course of a dispute in London between master tailors and their workmen, he had argued:

> The combinations of the men are but defensive measures resorted to for the purpose of counteracting the offensive ones of their masters… When every man knew that he could carry his labour to the highest bidder, there would be less motive for those combinations which now exist, and which exist because such combinations are the *only* means of redress they have. (Wallas 1898: 217)

In 1818, Place, along with other like-minded men such as Jeremy Bentham and Henry Bickersteth, decided to help fund a weekly publication called the *Gorgon* to raise public awareness on the subject. In retrospect, he believed that this publication was responsible for Joseph Hume espousing his project and observing in greater detail 'the operation and consequences of obnoxious laws' (Wallas 1898: 204–205). In this period, certain MPs began to be convinced of the need to repeal the laws. Place wrote to Benjamin Hobhouse and Thomas Hodgskin and finally, in 1822, Joseph Hume—a firm believer in *laissez-faire*—announced his intention of bringing a bill for the repeal of the laws against combinations before the House of Commons. Place, however, thought that the time was not yet ripe, or at least that Parliament was not yet ready for such a debate (Wallas 1898: 206). He was not alone in realising that it would be necessary to involve someone who would be able to authoritatively explain the need for this step. In the meantime, an increasing number of MPs had begun to question the efficacy and effects of the Combination Acts. The bill was presented in 1823 (Orth 1991: 68–69). Less than one year later, Place's requests for support had their first important result. In January 1824, John R. McCulloch, a disciple of David Ricardo, wrote an article for the *Edinburgh Review* supporting the proposed repeal and demonstrating the senselessness of the rules contained in the old Combination Act.[25]

> Wages like every thing else, ought always to be left to be regulated by the fair and free competition of the parties in the market, and ought never to be controlled by the interference of the Legislator. 'The property', says Dr Smith, 'which every man has in his own labour, as it is the original foundation of all other property, so it is the most sacred and inviolable. *The patrimony of a poor man lies in the strength and dexterity of his hands; and to hinder him from employing this strength and dexterity in what manner he thinks proper, without injury to his neighbours, is a plain violation of this most sacred property.*' But it is obviously false to affirm that workmen are allowed to dispose of their labour in any way they please, so long as they are prevented from concerting with each other the terms on which they are to sell it. Capacity to labour is to the poor man what stock is to the capitalist. But you would not prevent a hundred or a thousand capitalists from forming themselves into a company, or combination, who should take all their measures in common, and dispose of their property as they might, in their collective capacity, judge most advantageous for their interests: and why then should not a hundred or a thousand labourers be allowed to do the same by *their stock*? (McCulloch 1824: 318)

Recognising the workers' freedom to enjoy the fruits of their labour—nothing more than the sacrosanct right of property—while denying every

[25]As Place himself wrote: 'Its effect on many members was remarkable; several of them told me there was no resisting the conclusive arguments it contained, and one of them said he was prepared to speak the substance of the essay in the House' (Wallas 1898: 208). On McCulloch's opinion on the Combination Laws, see O'Brien (1970: 366–370).

one of them the possibility of pursuing their individual interest in association with other, similarly interested, people, was a blatant contradiction, not to say abject hypocrisy. There was actually more to it because, as Smith had suggested, in addition to the right of property and the complete freedom to dispose of it, the principle of equality was also in play. Just as no one could have dreamt of preventing a hundred or a thousand capitalists from joining their forces within a company, it was neither reasonable nor just to prohibit the workers from acting collectively. However, the idea of legalising economic conspiracies to allow the victims of the monopolistic attacks to defend themselves with the same weapons was not dead.

This particular passage from McCulloch's article contained a statement that concealed an outright mental revolution: the combination—which had always been a crime, associated with conspiracy—was candidly juxtaposed with the 'company', namely an economic entity deriving from a contract drawn up between two or more subjects to share a property, an activity, the inherent risks and, possibly, the profits.

Work—like everything else that could be bought and sold—had a price that was determined by the scarcity, the size of the demand and supply and the competition mechanism existing among both the workers and the capitalists. McCulloch took it as read that there was a 'natural and proper rate of wages' and also that the wages of a group of workers united (involved) in a combination could be aligned with this natural level or could be above or below it. When, for some reason, wages did not reach this level, the claims of the workers were more than fair and reasonable. Nevertheless, such claims were destined to be completely unheard and disregarded unless they were rendered explicit through a combination. Therefore, preventing the workers from adopting such strategies, and allowing their wages to be determined solely by the competition between their masters, went against good sense and against any notion of justice (McCulloch 1824: 319).[26] Conversely, in the case of workers

[26]'Not only, therefore, is a combination harmless in itself, but when it is entered into for the purpose of raising wages that have been unduly depressed, its object is most proper and desirable. No master ever willingly consents to raise wages; and the claim either of one or of a few individuals for an advance of wages is sure to be disregarded, so long as their fellows continue to work at the old rates. It is only when the whole, or the greater part of the workmen

deciding to resort to combination despite their wages being already at or above the natural level, then this could effectively be seen as improper and unreasonable. But this did not mean that a law against combinations was necessary and justified. If labour is a good like any other, or is considered such, why should those who dispose of it not be entitled to aspire to the highest price possible? Considering other commodities, any attempts to sell goods in the market were destined to come up against natural limits that could not be exceeded, even by resorting to the weapon of combination. Finally, McCulloch points out that practices such as '*forestalling* and *regrating*', aimed at manipulating the prices of commodities, have almost completely disappeared. Experience had by now shown that, despite allowing producers and dealers the greatest possible freedom of action, the markets continued to be supplied with every species of produce without any particular anomalies. Why, therefore, should it be thought that allowing workers the freedom to join forces to pursue their common interests should lead to such unpredictable or even perverse effects? (McCulloch 1824: 320). McCulloch was certain that if Parliament decided to take such a step it would not cause an upheaval in the labour market. Moreover, the very numbers involved made the prospect of huge groups of workers forming combinations unlikely, whereas for the masters—who were much fewer in number than the workers—such strategies were infinitely easier to implement. Therefore, in many respects, the much-debated Combination Acts tended to appear pointless, as well as unjust. Even reasoning for the sake of argument, there was nothing to suggest the contrary.

> Assuming, however, that the mass of workmen occasionally combine together, it appears absurd in the last degree to suppose that their combinations should ever enable them to obtain from their masters more than a due share of the produce of their labour. That the masters would resist a

belonging to a particular master or department of industry combine together, or when they act in that simultaneous manner which is in every respect equivalent to a combination, and refuse to continue to work without receiving an increase of wages, that it becomes the interest of the masters to comply with their demand. And hence it is obvious, that without the existence either of an open and avowed, or of a tacit and real combination, workmen would never be able to obtain a rise of wages by their own exertions, but would be left entirely dependent on the competition of their masters' (McCulloch 1824: 319).

> demand for any greater portion, is certain; and the slightest glance at the relative condition of the parties must satisfy every one that they cannot fail to succeed in defeating it. The workmen always suffer more from a *strike* than their masters. (McCulloch 1824: 321)

Adam Smith had said the same, and McCulloch saw fit to quote him on it. Although by this stage his repute as a friend of the poor was somewhat tarnished, evidently the picture he had painted in the *Wealth of Nations*—describing the oppression of the practically defenceless workers by the conspiracies of the capitalists—was still vivid and, more importantly, decidedly spendable in political terms. As McCulloch saw it, even if the combination weapon were to be taken up by the workers, the effects of their strategies would not only be irrelevant in themselves, but could also be easily nullified by the countermeasures of the masters. Every industrial sector had so many close allies that, even if it should be affected by a strike, it would be able to rely on the 'interested' solidarity of the masters of other sectors determined not to guarantee wages higher than those hitherto offered by their competitors. This meant that the workers involved in the combination would, in the end, be constrained to resume their previous occupation at the same wages that they had previously refused. The logical consequence of this was 'that a combination for an improper object, or to raise wages above their proper level, must cure itself—that it must necessarily bring its own chastisement along with it' (McCulloch 1824: 321–322). It was therefore improbable that the workers would decide to resort to a combination to obtain an increase in wages that any sensible person would consider 'unreasonable and exorbitant'. But even if this were to happen—if the workers were foolish enough to take up a cause that is patently 'unreasonable'—then their efforts are bound to be futile and ineffectual and would only expose them 'to great temporary hardship and distress' to find themselves ultimately obliged to accept 'the terms dictated by their masters' (McCulloch 1824: 322–323).

McCulloch's reasoning appeared to lead to the conclusion that the combinations of the workers were a corrective instrument only in cases where the level of wages was patently lower than it ought to be.[27] If a combination was successful and yielded the desired results, then it must have had right on its side. Moreover, what was just coincided with what it was possible to do and obtain based on the evolution of the economic process. This meant that the combination was an extremely expedient means both for eliminating contractual terms that were clearly unjust and for supporting the natural dynamic of the market as far as possible. And the truth of all this appeared all the more evident when one recalled what Smith had written apropos the conspiratorial strategies of the masters, which were 'tacit and unavowed' but just as powerful and efficient. In sum, for McCulloch there was nothing scandalous, reprehensible or unnatural in the combinations of the masters. It was a normal practice which no one could blame them for. What did, on the other hand, appear incomprehensible and profoundly unjust was to restrict these advantages to the capitalists alone and not also allow the workers to benefit from them: 'each party should be left, without any interference on the part of Government, to support their respective pretensions as they think best' (McCulloch 1824: 329). Regardless of the ethical and moral dimension, it was extremely counter-productive to permit or endorse a policy partial to the masters, which was what the Combination Acts had in effect brought about. Furthermore, it was far from certain that these laws were really favourable to the employers, and McCulloch surprisingly declared that he was convinced of exactly the opposite:

> Instead of that kind, conciliatory manner which a master ought always to exhibit towards the labourers in his employment, and which, were the latter relieved from restraint, he would always find it *for his advantage to exhibit*, the combination laws have done all that it was possible for any laws to do, to render him haughty, domineering, and capricious, to

[27]'Thus it appears, that if wages are at any time lower than they ought to be, a combination on the part of the workmen is highly proper and expedient, as being one of the best means of inducing their masters to raise them to their proper level. But if wages have already reached their natural limits, the self-interest of the masters will induce them to resist the combination, and the workmen will not obtain another farthing. The laws to prevent combinations are, therefore, either unnecessary, or unjust and injurious. They are unnecessary, whenever the rate of wages is as high as circumstances will permit; and they are unjust and injurious whenever it is below that level' (McCulloch 1824: 323).

> impress him with a conviction that he is of a superior *caste*, and that the labouring poor neither have, nor ought to have, the same rights as himself. The poor are sensible of this ignominious treatment, and they naturally and deeply resent it. The combination laws have taught both masters and workmen to believe, that there is one measure of justice for the rich and another for the poor. They have thus set the interests and the feelings of these two great classes in direct and hostile opposition to each other; and have, in consequence, done more to engender a deadly hatred between the different orders of society—to turn the masters into petty despots, and the workmen into treacherous and rebellious slaves, than can be easily conceived or imagined by those who are not pretty intimately acquainted with the state of society in the manufacturing districts. (McCulloch 1824: 330)

At the end of the day, the climate of conflict that these laws had created was not beneficial to anyone. Even leaving aside the inherent injustice, it was obvious how damaging they were in terms of political and economic utility. Chaining up the giants had done nothing but fuel their anger and their strength: in the end, this was the argument that had to convince.[28] Paradoxically, no one really wanted to pave the way for them, not even those who were defending their interests. The idea was that once they were freed they would end up losing vitality and even their raison d'être. In other words, recognising the freedom of creatures who had always been seen as threatening and whose presence was by now looming was seen as a way of neutralising the principal passion—namely, hatred—which was the source of the conflict, and also of depriving the conflict of the soul that kept it alive. The economic effects and benefits for society as a whole would soon be visible. If the giants were left free to address each other on equal terms, without constrictions on either side, perhaps wages would return to a natural level, following the competitive logic of the market (as Smith had imagined?).

---

[28]This is the observation ultimately made by Place: 'The laws against combinations were inimical to the working people in many respects. They induced them to break and disregard the laws. They made them suspect the intentions of every man who tendered his services. They made them hate their employers with a rancour which nothing else could have produced. And they made them hate those of their own class who refused to join them, to such an extent as cordially to seek to do them mischief' (Wallas 1898: 239).

Nevertheless, as Thompson noted (1991: 563), there was something paradoxical about the fact that violence on the one hand, and secrecy on the other, were playing a decisive role in strengthening the arguments of those who had been battling for the repeal of the Combination Acts. However, the optimistic attitude with which the battle to raise public awareness was fought both inside and outside Parliament was very evident, and the weakness of the position of those opposing it was equally evident.

In June 1824, the bill determining the abolition of the Combination Acts was passed first in the House of Commons and then in the House of Lords: 'the celerity of passage was due to the absence of debate' (Orth 1991: 75).[29]

Had society finally been freed from the threat of conspiracy? As McCulloch, Place and those who had adhered to their ideas saw it, the antibodies necessary for defence against what was none other than a natural disease aggravated by the wrong treatment had certainly been set in circulation, and the strength of society would allow it to restore its lost equilibrium.[30] It is hard to say how much there was in the words of McCulloch (and Ricardo), of what Smith had posed as an issue, without pontificating anything and without suggesting legislative measures. What was definitely implied in their observations, albeit unnoticed, was the old principle of *monopolium vs. monopolium*. It had finally begun to make headway, maybe definitively, but its appearance had changed. It had been stripped (though not completely) of its moral and political weapons and dressed in another suit of armour, apparently less vulnerable because tailored to a new style, more attentive to the new interpretation and closer to the recent discovery of the truth.

In June 1825, a year after the abolition of the Combination Acts, Place wrote to Burdett, disclosing the great trust he had in the natural effects of this virtuous rationale:

[29]According to Arthur Aspinall (1949: XXV), Place's efforts would have been in vain if Parliament had not taken Smith's ideas into due consideration in the interim.

[30]According to William D. Grampp (1979: 506), Place's arguments did not entirely coincide with those of McCulloch, who insisted above all on the fact that competition would render the combinations peaceful and relatively ineffective.

> Combinations will soon cease to exist. Men have been kept together for long periods only by the oppression of the laws; these being repealed, combinations will lose the matter which cements them into masses, and they will fall to pieces. All will be as orderly as even a Quaker could desire. He knows nothing of the working people who can suppose that, when left at liberty to act for themselves, without being driven into permanent associations by the oppression of the laws, they will continue to contribute money for distant and doubtful experiments, for uncertain and precarious benefits. Even now in a very populous part of the country, and where the people are particularly ill treated, the men have refused to contribute a penny each per week to pay the expense of a delegate to be sent to London. If let alone, combinations, excepting now and then, and for particular purposes, under peculiar circumstances, will cease to exist. (Wallas 1898: 217–218)

Once the laws that forbade them were abolished, the combinations would lose the adhesive that kept them together, the same adhesive that cemented the masses. Once liberty had made them disappear, amazingly the world would become so well-ordered that even a Quaker would be able to find no fault with it. To tell the truth, order—which was already a great deal in terms of results—was not the only positive repercussion that, in time, everyone would become aware of. Simultaneously, great commercial prosperity would emerge, because there would be no more of the strikes or other forms of protest that had caused grave losses by reducing the country's productive capacity.[31] In this scenario, competition would indeed bear fruit. It seemed almost a certainty. Abolishing the combination laws, and allowing workers and capitalists to act collectively if they wished, was the only way of placing the labour market in a condition of 'free and unrestrained competition' (McCulloch 1824: 331–332).[32] Looking closer at this reasoning, as McCulloch had done, revealed that it was the mechanism of competition that would make the combinations ineffective, or in any case, harmless (Grampp 1979: 506).

---

[31] As Place noted: 'From one end of the country to the other masters and men were engaged in industrial conflict' (Wallas 1898: 218).

[32] On this passage, William D. Grampp (1979: 506).

The main certainty of the liberal dream was already taking shape: a general disease did not require a general remedy because it would cure itself (Orth 1991: 70).

Self-Regulating Society: The Giants Take Each Other Out

The idea that combinations were 'powerless' in a competitive free market regime had already been expressed by David Ricardo.[33] Some years earlier in a letter to McCulloch (4 December 1820), he stated that 'the true remedy for combinations is perfect liberty on both sides, and adequate protection against violence and outrage' (Ricardo 2004: VIII, 316).[34] Moreover, he also maintained that these laws did not protect either the capitalists from the conspiratorial attacks of the workers, or the workers from the conspiratorial attacks of the capitalists.[35]

Beyond these short private notes written by his master, McCulloch was the only classical economist to exert himself for the abolition of the combination laws. It is, effectively, disconcerting and hard to understand why the issue did not attract the interest of this group of intellectuals (Grampp 1979: 506–509). In view of this, perhaps we have to ask ourselves if it really was a victory of classical economics. Clearly, it is hard to imagine that the Parliament in which the policy was matured was unaware of the new convictions being developed by the economists, and emerging more specifically from Benthamite ideology (Dicey 2008: 139).

---

[33]Although his vision of society was not marked by the presence of a mechanism that ensured 'the mutual compatibility of individual interests'; instead it was 'one of the potential conflicts between the productive classes of a capitalist system' (Milgate and Stimson 2009: 52).

[34]This passage of the letter is also quoted by Grampp (1979: 506).

[35]Nevertheless, 'by the standard of fairness the laws were objectionable because while they fell on employers, they fell more heavily on workers' (Grampp 1979: 515). Moreover, as noted by Milgate and Stimson (2009: 53): 'In practical and policy terms, Ricardo became convinced that the general character of society was, in the short run, one of an inherent conflict between the classes, over which the government and the statesman could exercise little or no direct role in ameliorating the inconveniences. They must rely instead on the long-run workings of the market mechanism'.

On the other hand, it cannot be ruled out that Parliament acted independently of these, driven substantially by pure and expedient pragmatism (Grampp 1979: 515).

That said, the new legislation overturned the order established twenty-five years earlier and, at the same time, swept under the carpet an extremely lengthy legal tradition dating back a full century. In fact, the Acts of 1799–1800 followed a line of legislative production that first made its appearance in the 1720s. Through the 1824 Act, the British Parliament repealed all the laws on combinations: 'its principal object of freeing combinations from prosecution for conspiracy was plainly achieved'; and, in restating the principle of equality, even the combinations between capitalists (conceived 'as mirror images of combinations of workmen') were declared to be not actionable (Orth 1991: 78, 79).[36]

Drawing back the ideological veil that cloaked and probably sustained this political decision, certain questions were still on the table. Was this Act really intended to establish free trade in labour? Did it really give expression 'to the idea that the sale or purchase of labour should be as entirely a matter of free contract as the purchase of boots or shoes'? (Dicey 1904: 520)[37] Did the policy of allowing capitalists and workers to plot against each other really protect the ideal of a free market operating through the logic of competition?

Although the abolition of the combination laws has been presented as the triumph of classical economics, it was anomalous in that the effect was a reduction of competition in the labour market.[38] While it can be assumed that liberalism made a major contribution to the rule on which the new-born labour market was structured, it was nevertheless done employing the old conspiracy rationale which had for centuries

[36]'Thus far, the 1824 Act was negative only: it swept away all the laws (common as well as statute) on combination and conspiracy' (Orth 1991: 79).

[37]According to the liberal jurist, the act of repealing gave expression to two convictions: 'the one is the belief that trade in labour ought to be as free as any other kind of trade; the other is the well-grounded conviction that there ought to be one and the same law for men as for masters' (Dicey 1904: 522). See also Dicey (2008: 137–138).

[38]According to William D. Grampp, the influence of economists 'although noticeable, was small'. There were indeed 'three other groups that influenced the event much more: one was the leadership of political parties, especially the Tory; another was the radical reformers; the third was the working class' (Grampp 1979: 501).

been considered violent and destructive of the liberty of the economic actors and of the mythical mechanism of fair competition on which the market was based. The combination laws were repealed by making explicit reference to the logic of competition and defending its principle. Basically, this stance was grounded on the old precept which held that, faced by a conspiracy manipulating the natural price-setting dynamics, recourse to the same (illegal and immoral) weapons as the conspirators was the only defence. All this had no real connection with the solicitation or defence of competition. Combinations were the oldest way of altering the process of setting the value of goods, considered as the natural result of the match played by sellers and buyers. For Adam Smith, 'competition ensured that market participants would not have the power to make agreements to set prices'; he defined competition 'negatively, as the absence of power to influence price', as 'the absence of monopoly or combination' (Nockleby 1994: 459).[39] Consequently, as has been pointed out, 'a modern reader might be puzzled by calling the struggle between laborers and their employers competition. This type of relationship in modern economics might be thought of as conflict or rivalry, but not competition' (Nockleby 1994: 460).

Behind the legitimisation of the conspiracies of workers and employers was a new concept of the market; this was based, not on the new principle of free competition, but on another older rationale founded on the right of resistance and borrowed from political thought through the legitimising reflections of moralists.

Immediately following the repeal of the hated laws, the certainty that acknowledgement of the freedom of all workers and all capitalists to act in concert with others would defuse the conflict and deprive the combinations of their strength and vitality began to teeter. Or rather, it was not borne out by the facts. As Thompson put it, 'for a brief period, several unions looked with favour upon Place's gospel of the common interests of workers and employers. But the theory of class collaboration had scarcely made its appearance before it came under fire, first from the

[39]As has been pointed out by Samuel Hollander (1973: 126), 'Accordingly, the Smithian conception of competition must be carefully distinguished from the modern conception which envisages sellers (and consumers) as *price takers* rather than *price makers*' (italics mine).

Trades Newspaper, and, second, from the Owenite Socialists' (Thompson 1991: 569). The new giants not only demonstrated that they had no intention of collaborating, nor any interest in doing so, but grasped the new opportunities and new margins to give fresh fuel to the conflict. So much so that, in the winter of 1824–1825, the employers petitioned both houses 'to re-enact the old laws or to devise some new and even more drastic legislation' (Wallas 1898: 218). Fully aware and concerned about what was happening, Place and Hume immediately took action so that the petitions would be withdrawn, but no great efforts were called for. The restoration of the pre-1824 situation had no political allure, while the reaction of the workers to any such hypothesis was powerful and at times violent (Thomspon 1991: 569; Orth 1991: 85). This was the context in which the famous work by Thomas Hodgskin, *Labour Defended Against the Claims of Capital* appeared, the nexus of which was found just a few pages from the beginning: 'Combination is of itself no crime; on the contrary it is the principle on which societies are held together' (Hodgskin 1825: 4).

Hodgskin—the *Smithian anarchist*[40]—went straight to the heart of the matter and expressed it succinctly and effectively, possibly even going beyond his own intentions. Under the new light he chose to observe it by, the big question seemed almost skewed. Up until then, the term combination had been used to describe generically any behaviour in which a group of people employed a conspiratorial strategy to pursue certain economic interests, a strategy which also created unfair relations of complicity and violated the bond of trust that held society together. Phenomena of this kind were considered potentially subversive—and, therefore, dangerous and actionable—partly because they often ended up creating giants that were potentially tyrannical and impossible to stand up to: first and foremost those with monopolistic ambitions. Now, people had finally realised that it was society itself that generated such creatures through its economic dynamics, and that these phenomena could be stopped only at the cost of violating inalienable principles. It was not a

[40]According to the well-known epithet given to him by Terence W. Hutchison (1978: 242). On this thinker, I refer to the now classic David Stack (1998). For a critical reading of Hodgskin not toeing the line of his classic image of Ricardian socialist, I refer to Alberto Mingardi (2018).

question of disease, but simply of the movement of society, which spontaneously organised itself into groups around specific issues.

How could a rationale that held society together be criminalised? On the other hand, accepting it meant abandoning one of the fundamental principles governing the societies of the *Ancien Régime*. This principle had behind it a wealth of literature derived from both theological-moral thought and legal-political knowledge, and had always been called up to defend communities and states from threatening forms of conspiracy. Nevertheless, it was undeniable that for some time this same principle had been transformed into one of the main weapons used in English policy to keep at bay a new world seething with entirely unforeseeable potential. This was why, in response to the workers' demands, some people thought it useful to restore this principle to life so as not to leave the field open to forces that appeared gigantic not only for the capitalists but for political order as a whole. Stripped of the competition mechanism, the labour market began to show its political face:

> No other combination seems unjust or mischievous, in the view of government, but our combinations to obtain a proper reward for our labour. It is heinous crime in the eyes of a legislature, composed exclusively of capitalists and landlords, and representing no other interests than their own, for us to try, by any means, to obtain for ourselves, and for the comfortable subsistence of our families, a larger share of our own produce than these our masters choose to allow us. All the moral evils that ever plagued a society have been anticipated by the Ministers from our persevering in our claims. To put down combination they have departed from principles held sacred for upwards of two hundred years. They have made also a law handing us over to the magistrates like vagabonds and thieves, and we are to be condemned almost unheard, and without the privilege and formality of a public trial. All that we are compelled to suffer, all that we have had inflicted on us, has been done for the advantage of capital. (Hodgskin 1825: 4)

In Hodgskin's harsh denunciation, the echo of the contemptuous words used by Smith half a century earlier in the first book of the *Wealth of Nations* was all too clear. It also resonated with the attack made by Thelwall thirty years earlier on the English government for taking the side of the new-born capitalist culture in its establishment of new power relations. While at the time this attack had appeared visionary and unyoked from reality, it had now acquired the savour of a terrible prophecy.

In fighting his battle Hodgskin had come extremely close to what was labelled as 'liberal' thought.[41] At the same time his reasoning appeared to conceal something else. Combination had at length been considered a crime, but to his eyes it was nothing more than the social mechanism that shaped human coexistence, organising it on opposing fronts. Legitimising the rationale of combination meant embracing the idea that it was just (if not necessary) to allow a monopolist dynamic to be neutralised or offset by another dynamic of the same nature. This idea, which had seen the light thirty years earlier, had survived despite all the doubt, resistance and silence. It was clear how closely Hodgskin's reasoning followed that of McCulloch in this line of thought. As pointed out by Thompson, 'he was primarily concerned with removing those malignly created obstructions which caused the market economy to malfunction'; and even his support 'for trade unions was given in the expectation that their activity would redress the disperate bargaining strenght of labourers and capitalists and this contribute to a more perfect functioning of the market' (Thompson 1984: 98). At the same time, Hodgskin also emphasised just how wrong Place was. Sanctioning the freedom to conspire had not eliminated the conflict; rather, it had institutionalised it. Or possibly it had, ultimately, harnessed it to the rationale of collective bargaining.

And what about Smith's teachings? Were Hodgskin's arguments a logical consequence of them? Undoubtedly association was a natural right, as was that of defence/resistance. And in the case of the workers' combinations these two rights overlapped, or were indivisible. For this reason too, combinations were not a criminal offence and it was neither possible nor logical to criminalise them. They were, on the contrary, a sign

[41]As has been pointed out by Noel Thompson (1998: 46), 'what strikes one immediately about these works [*Labour Defended Against the Claims of Capital*, 1825; *Popular Political Economy, Four Lectures Delivered and the London Mechanics' Institute*, 1827; *The Natural and Artificial Rights of Property Contrasted*, 1832] is the extent to which they embraced the concepts and analytical devices of classical political economy'. But we must also say that Hodgskin 'rejected the Malthus-Ricardo idea that wages were kept at subsistence level through the operation of the principle of population—it was not natural in any sense. He instead located the problem squarely in the domain of social regulation' (Milgate and Stimson 2009: 232).

of the vitality of society which shaped itself in a natural and spontaneous manner. They also had the important additional merit of holding society together. At the end of the day, it was through combinations that society demonstrated its capacity to regulate itself, producing the cement required to resist disintegrative impulses. In other words, it was the proof that it could maintain order on its own.

On the one hand, this idea brought with it the collapse of the ideal of creating the best possible order determined by a regulatory political authority. On the other hand, it revealed the foundering of a society conceived in a utopian manner as the result of a harmonious network of individually pursued trajectories. The idea that the market could disintegrate society and, in so doing, render it harmless, had proved unrealistic. Those who believed it were ingenuous and probably went much further than Smith's actual words. Without ever losing sight of the realism that made him pragmatic, Smith had in fact never undervalued the limitations of a society sustained by market logic. All forms of aggregation entailed a violation of the rules of the competitive game, and such infringements obstructed the creation of the longed-for social harmony. The limitations had to be taken into account. Perhaps society would never become either sufficiently fluid or sufficiently fragmented to be in harmony, precisely because the interests that fuelled it were often united in conspiratorial forms that were at the origin of the conflicts.

In sum, Smith's obsession with the monopolist threat, and with strategies aimed either at seeking political complicity or at fraudulently overcoming the competition mechanism, implied the notion that, for the market to survive, interests had to be pursued individually without entering into cahoots. Now, finally, this idea had apparently found a corollary: each social cluster generated by the conspiracy and complicity sought by groups of individuals could—or perhaps had to—be offset only if it came up against another group determined to resort to a similar conspiratorial strategy and legitimised to do so. This was the only way in which, not only the market, but the whole of society could be seen as a self-sufficient and self-regulating organism. Fideistically for some, and realistically for others, the entities emerging from this movement had to be allowed to act against and resist each other. Beyond this, one had simply to hope and trust that the clashes of the giants would never lead to definitive conflicts but to worlds of power relations tending towards utopian equilibrium.

References

Aspinall, A. 1949. *The Early English Trade Unions. Documents from the Home Office Papers in the Public Record Office*. London: The Batchworth Press.

Caeys, G. 1994. The Origins of the Rights of Labor: Republicans, Commerce, and the Construction of Modern Social Theory in Britain, 1796–1805. *The Journal of Modern History* 66 (2): 249–290.

Dicey, A.V. 1904. The Combination Laws as Illustrating the Relation Between Law and Opinion in England During the Nineteenth Century. *Harvard Law Review* 17 (8): 511–532.

Dicey, A.V. 2008 [1914]. *Lectures on the Relation Between Law and Public Opinion in England During the Nineteenth Century*. Indianapolis: Liberty Fund.

Eden, F.M. 1797. *The State of the Poor. Or an History of the Labouring Classes in England, from the Conquest to the Present Period*, 3 vols. London: Egerton, Bremner, White, Davis, Payne, Robinson, Debrett, Faulder.

George, M.D. 1936. Revisions in Economic History: IV. The Combination Laws. *The Economic History Review* 6 (2): 172–178.

Ginzberg, E. 2002 [1934]. *Adam Smith and the Founding of Market Economics*. New Brunswick and London: Transaction Publishers.

Grampp, W.D. 1979. The Economists and the Combination Laws. *The Quarterly Journal of Economics* 93 (4): 501–522.

Hampsher-Monk, I. 1991. John Thelwall and the Eighteenth-Century Radical Response to Political Economy. *The Historical Journal* 34 (I): 1–20.

Hampsher-Monk, I. 2006. British Radicalism and the Anti-Jacobins. In *The Cambridge History of Eighteenth-Century Political Thought*, ed. M. Goldie and R. Wokler, 660–687. Cambridge: Cambridge University Press.

Hodgskin, T. 1825. *Labour Defended Against the Claims of Capital*. London: Knight and Lacey; Edinburgh: Baynes; Glasgow: M'Phun; Dublin: Westley and Tyrrel.

Hollander, S. (1973). *The Economics of Adam Smith*. London and Toronto: Heinemann Educational Books/University of Toronto Press.

Hutchison, T.W. 1978. *On Revolutions and Progress in Economic Knowledge*. Cambridge: Cambridge University Press.

McCulloch, J.R. 1824. Combination Laws—Restraints on Emigration, etc. *Edinburgh Review* XXXIX: 315–345.

Milgate, M., and S.C. Stimson. 2009. *After Adam Smith: A Century of Transformation in Politics and Political Economy*. Princeton, NJ and Oxford: Princeton University Press.

Mingardi, A. 2018. Thomas Hodgskin, Rational Optimist. *Economic Affairs* 38 (1): 38–57.
Moher, J. 1988. From Suppression to Containment: Roots of Trade Union Law to 1825. In *British Trade Unionism, 1750–1850. The Formative Years,* ed. J. Rule, 74–97. London and New York: Longman.
Nockleby, J.T. 1994. Two Theories of Competition in the Early 19th Century Labor Cases. *The American Journal of Legal History* 38 (4): 452–481.
O'Brien, D.P. 1970. *J.M. McCulloch. A Study in Classical Economics.* London: Allen & Unwin.
Orth, J.V. 1991. *Combination and Conspiracy. A Legal History of Trade Unionism, 1721–1906.* Oxford: Clarendon Press.
Polanyi, K. 1944. *The Great Transformation. The Political and Economic Origins of Our Time.* New York and Toronto: Rinehart & Company.
Ricardo, D. 2004 [1951–1973]. *Letters, 1819–June 1821.* In *The Works and Correspondence of David Ricardo,* 11 vols., vol. 8, ed. P. Sraffa, with the collaboration of M.H. Dobb. Indianapolis: Liberty Fund.
Rothschild, E. 2001. *Economic Sentiments. Adam Smith, Condorcet and the Enlightenment.* London and Cambridge, MA: Harvard University Press.
Stack, D. 1998. *Nature and Artifice. The Life and Thought of Thomas Hodgskin (1787–1869).* Woodbridge: Boydell.
Thelwall, J. 1796. *The Rights of Nature, Against the Usurpations of Establishments,* Letter I. London: Symonds and March.
Thompson, E.P. 1991 [1963]. *The Making of the English Working Class.* London: Penguin.
Thompson, N.W. 1984. *The People's Science. The Popular Political Economy of Exploitation and Crisis 1816–34.* Cambridge: Cambridge University Press.
Thompson, N. 1998. *The Real Rights of Man. Political Economies for the Working Class 1775–1850.* London and Sterling, VA: Pluto Press.
Trevelyan, G.M. 1922. *British History in the Nineteenth Century and After (1782–1919).* London, New York, and Toronto: Longman.
Wallas, G. 1898. *The Life of Francis Place, 1771–1854.* London, New York, and Bombay: Longman.
Webb, S., and B. Webb. 1911 [1898]. *The History of Trade Unionism.* London: Longman.
Willis, K. 1979. The Role in Parliament of the Economic Ideas of Adam Smith, 1776–1800. *History of Political Economy* 11 (4): 505–544.

Bibliography

Althusius, J. 1614. *Politica methodicè digesta atque exemplis sacris & profanis illustrata*. Herbornæ Nassoviorum: Corvini.

Alvey, J.E. 2003. *Adam Smith: Optimist or Pessimist? A New Problem Concerning the Teleological Basis of Commercial Society*. Aldershot: Taylor & Francis.

Anderson, E. 2016. Adam Smith on Equality. In *Adam Smith. His Life, Thought, and Legacy*, ed. R.P. Hanley, 157–172. Princeton, NJ and Oxford: Princeton University Press.

Appleby, J.O. 1978. *Economic Thought and Ideology in Seventeenth-Century England*. Princeton, NJ: Princeton University Press.

Aspinall, A. 1949. *The Early English Trade Unions. Documents from the Home Office Papers in the Public Record Office*. London: The Batchworth Press.

Avendano (de), D. 1668–1675. *Thesaurus indicus, seu generalis instructor pro regimine conscientiae, in iis quae ad Indias spectant*, 5 vols. Antverpiae: Meursium.

Bañes, D. 1595. *Decisiones de iure & iustitia*. Venetiis: Minima Societate.

Barry, N. 1990. Adam Smith and the Ethics of Capitalism. In *Adam Smith's Legacy. His Thought in Our Time*, ed. N. Elliott, 92–100. London: Adam Smith Institute.

R. Rosolino, *Countervailing Powers*,
https://doi.org/10.1007/978-3-030-37802-8

Bhanu Mehta, P. 2006. Self-Interest and Other Interests. In *The Cambridge Companion to Adam Smith*, ed. K. Haakonssen, 246–269. Cambridge and New York: Cambridge University Press.

Bodin, J. 1997 [1568]. *Response to the paradoxes of Malestroit*, trans. and ed. H. Tudor and R.W. Dyson. Bristol: University of Durham—Thoemmes Press.

Bonacina, M. 1632a [1619]. *De contractibus*. In M. Bonacina, *Opera omnia*, 3 vols., Tomo II. Antverpiae: Meursium.

Bonacina, M. 1632b [1627]. *De Simonia*. In M. Bonacina, *Opera omnia*, 3 vols., Tomo I. Antverpiae: Meursium.

Botero, G. 1956 [1598]. *The Reason of State*, trans. P.J. Waley and D.P. Waley with an Introduction by D.P. Waley. New Haven, CT: Yale University Press.

Boucoyannis, D. 2013. The Equalizing Hand: Why Adam Smith Thought the Market Should Produce Wealth Without Steep Inequality. *Perspectives on Politics* 11 (4): 1051–1070.

Bourdieu, P. 2014 [2012]. *On the State. Lectures at the Collège de France, 1989–1992*, ed. P. Champagne, R. Lenoir, F. Poupeau, and M.-C. Rivière. Cambridge: Polity.

Braudel, F. 1977. *Afterthoughts on Material Civilisation and Capitalism*. Baltimore: John Hopkins University Press.

Braudel, F. 1982 [1979]. *Civilization and Capitalism, 15th–18th Century*, Vol. II: *The Wheels of Commerce*. London: William Collins Sons & Co.

Brubaker, L. 2006. Does the 'Wisdom of Nature' Need Help? In *New Voices on Adam Smith*, ed. L. Montes and E. Schlisser, 168–192. London and New York: Routledge.

Caeys, G. 1994. The Origins of the Rights of Labor: Republicans, Commerce, and the Construction of Modern Social Theory in Britain, 1796–1805. *The Journal of Modern History* 66 (2): 249–290.

Chancellor, E. 1999. *Devil Take the Hindmost. A History of Financial Speculation*. London: Macmillan.

Ciazzi, A. 1630. *Disceptationes forenses criminales ad reorum defensam*. Maceratae: Bonomi.

Clark, C.M.A. 1988. Natural Law Influences on Adam Smith. *Quaderni di Storia dell'Economia Politica* 6 (3): 59–86.

Coase, R.H. 1976. Adam Smith's View of Man. *Journal of Law and Economics* 19 (3): 529–546.

Cohen, E.S. 1989. Justice and Political Economy in Commercial Society: Adam Smith's 'Science of a Legislator'. *The Journal of Politics* 51 (1): 50–72.

Cohn, G. 1895. Competition and Combination. *The Economic Journal* 20: 550–562.

Condorcet, J.A.N. 1847–1849a [1795]. *Esquisse d'un tableau historique des progrès de l'esprit humain* (*Fragment de l'Histoire de la Xe époque*). In *Œuvres de Condorcet, publiées par A. Condorcet O'Connor et F. Arago*, 12 vols., vol. 6. Paris: Didot.

Condorcet, J.A.N. 1847–1849b [1775]. *Monopole et monopoleur.* In *Œuvres de Condorcet, publiées par A. Condorcet O'Connor et F. Arago*, 12 vols., vol. 11. Paris: Didot.

Condorcet, J.A.N. 1847–1849c [1776]. *Réflexions sur le commerce de blés.* In *Œuvres de Condorcet, publiées par A. Condorcet O'Connor et F. Arago*, 12 vols., vol. 11. Paris: Didot.

Cremaschi, S. 1989. Adam Smith. Skeptical Newtonianism, Disenchanted Republicanism, and the Birth of Social Science. In *Knowledge and Politics: Case Studies on the Relationship Between Epistemology and Political Philosophy*, ed. M. Dascal and O. Gruengard, 83–110. Boulder, CO: Westview.

Deciano, T. 1590. *Tractatus criminalis*, 2 vols. Venetiis: Zenarios.

Decock, W. 2013. *Theologians and Contract Law. The Moral Transformation of the Ius Commune (ca. 1500–1650).* Leiden and Boston: Martinus Nijhoff.

De Roover, R. 1974a [1951]. Monopoly Theory Prior to Adam Smith: A Revision. In R. De Roover, *Business, Banking and Economic Thought in Late Medieval and Early Modern Europe*, ed. J. Kirshner, 273–305. Chicago and London: University of Chicago Press.

De Roover, R. 1974b [1955]. Scholastic Economics. Survival and Lasting Influence from the Sixteenth Century to Adam Smith. In R. De Roover, *Business, Banking and Economic Thought in Late Medieval and Early Modern Europe*, ed. J. Kirshner, 306–335. Chicago and London: University of Chicago Press.

Dicastillo, I. 1641. *De iustitia et iure*, 2 vols. Antverpiae: Trognæsium.

Dicey, A.V. 1904. The Combination Laws as Illustrating the Relation Between Law and Opinion in England During the Nineteenth Century. *Harvard Law Review* 17 (8): 511–532.

Dicey, A.V. 2008 [1914]. *Lectures on the Relation Between Law and Public Opinion in England During the Nineteenth Century.* Indianapolis: Liberty Fund.

Dickinson, H.T. 1994. *The Politics of the People in Eighteenth-Century Britain.* New York: St. Martin's Press.

Dorfman, J. 1946. *The Economic Mind in American Civilization, 1606*–1865, 2 vols. New York: The Viking Press.

Duret, J. 1583. *Traicté des peines et amendes, tant pour les materies Criminelles que Civiles.* Lyon: Rigaud.

Eden, F.M. 1797. *The State of the Poor. Or an History of the Labouring Classes in England, from the Conquest to the Present Period*, 3 vols. London: Egerton, Bremner, White, Davis, Payne, Robinson, Debrett, Faulder.

Elliott, J.E. 2000. Adam Smith's Conceptualization of Power, Markets and Politics. *Review of Social Economy* 58 (4): 429–454.
Evensky, J. 2005a. *Adam Smith's Moral Philosophy. A Historical and Contemporary Perspective on Markets, Law, Ethics, and Culture.* Cambridge: Cambridge University Press.
Evensky, J. 2005b. Adam Smith's 'Theory of Moral Sentiments': On Morals and Why They Matter to a Liberal Society of Free People and Free Markets. *The Journal of Economic Perspectives* 19 (3): 109–130.
Fagundez, S. 1641. *De iustitia et contractibus.* Lugduni: Anisson et Boissat.
Fairlamb, H.L. 1996. Smith's Other Hand: A Capitalist Theory of Exploitation. *Social Theory and Practice* 22 (2): 193–223.
Farinacci, P. 1621. *De immunitate ecclesiarum et confugientibus ad eas.* Romae: ex Typographia Reverendæ Cameræ Apostolicæ.
Fleischacker, S. 2004. *On Adam Smith's Wealth of Nations. A Philosophical Companion.* Princeton, NJ and Oxford: Princeton University Press.
Fleischacker, S. 2005. *A Short History of Distributive Justice.* Cambridge, MA and London: Harvard University Press.
Fleischacker, S. 2013. Adam Smith on Equality. In *Oxford Handbook of Adam Smith*, ed. C.J. Berry, M.P. Paganelli, and C. Smith, 485–500. Oxford: Oxford University Press.
Forbes, D. 1966. *Introduction.* In A. Ferguson, *An Essay on the History of Civil Society*, edited with an Introduction by D. Forbes. Edinburgh: Edinburgh University Press.
Forbes, D. 1975. Sceptical Whiggism, Commerce and Liberty. In *Essays on Adam Smith*, ed. A.S. Skinner and T. Wilson, 179–201. Oxford: Clarendon Press.
Force, P. 2003. *Self-Interest Before Adam Smith. A Genealogy of Economic Science.* Cambridge and New York: Cambridge University Press.
Fox-Genovese, E. 1976. *The Origin of Physiocracy. Economic Revolution and Social Order in Eighteenth-Century France.* Ithaca and London: Cornell University Press.
Fritsch, A. 1659. *Commentatio synoptica ad nobilissimam legem unicam cod. de monopoliis.* Janae: Sengenwaldi.
Galbraith, J.K. 1956 [1952]. *American Capitalism. The Concept of Countervailing Power.* Harmondsworth: Penguin.
García, F. 1583. *Del tratado utilissimo y muy general de todos los contractos, quantos en los negocios humanos se suelen offrecer*, 2 vols. Valencia: Navarro.
George, M.D. 1936. Revisions in Economic History: IV. The Combination Laws. *The Economic History Review* 6 (2): 172–178.

Ginzberg, E. 2002 [1934]. *Adam Smith and the Founding of Market Economics.* New Brunswick and London: Transaction Publishers.
Ginzburg, C. 2018. Casuistry and Irony: Some Reflections on Pascal's Provinciales. In *A Historical Approach to Casuistry. Norms and Exceptions in a Comparative Perspective*, ed. C. Ginzburg and L. Biasiori, 282–300. London: Bloomsbury.
Grampp, W.D. 1979. The Economists and the Combination Laws. *The Quarterly Journal of Economics* 93 (4): 501–522.
Grassis (de), C. 1617. *Tractatus de Effectibus Amicitiae.* Panormi: Maringum.
Grenier, J.-Y. 1996. *L'économie d'Ancien Régime. Un monde de l'échange et de l'incertitude.* Paris: Albin Michel.
Groenewegen, P.D. 2002a [1983]. Turgot, Beccaria and Smith. In P.D. Groenewegen, *Eighteenth-Century Economics. Turgot, Beccaria and Their Contemporaries*, 3–47. London and New York: Routledge.
Groenewegen, P.D. 2002b [1998]. Boisguilbert and Eighteenth-Century Economics. In P.D. Groenewegen, *Eighteenth-Century Economics. Turgot, Beccaria and Their Contemporaries*, 111–124. London and New York: Routledge.
Groenewegen, P.D. 2002c [1969]. Turgot and Adam Smith. In P.D. Groenewegen, *Eighteenth-century Economics. Turgot, Beccaria and Their Contemporaries*, 363–378. London and New York: Routledge.
Grotius, H. 2005 [1625]. *The Rights of War and Peace*, 3 vols., ed. and with an Introduction by R. Tuck. Indianapolis: Liberty Fund.
Guery, A. 2011. *Introduction. De Montchrestien à Cantillon: de l'économie politique à l'analyse économique.* In *Montchrestien et Cantillon. Le commerce et l'émergence d'une pensée économique*, sous la direction de A. Guery, 7–55. Paris: ENS.
Guyot, M. 1785. *Répertoire universel et raisonné de jurisprudence civile, criminelle, canonique et beneficiale*, 28 vols. Paris: Visse.
Haakonssen, K. 1981. *The Science of Legislator. The Natural Jurisprudence of David Hume and Adam Smith.* Cambridge: Cambridge University Press.
Haakonssen, K. 1996. *Natural Law and Moral Philosophy. From Grotius to the Scottish Enlightenment.* Cambridge: Cambridge University Press.
Haakonssen, K. 2016. The Lectures on Jurisprudence. In *Adam Smith. His Life, Thought, and Legacy*, ed. R.P. Hanley, 48–66. Princeton, NJ and Oxford: Princeton University Press.
Halévy, E. 1928. *The Growth of Philosophic Radicalism.* London: Faber & Faber.
Hamowy, R. 1987. *The Scottish Enlightenment and the Theory of Spontaneous Order.* Carbondale and Edwardsville: Southern Illinois University Press.
Hampsher-Monk, I. 1991. John Thelwall and the Eighteenth-Century Radical Response to Political Economy. *The Historical Journal* 34 (I): 1–20.

Hampsher-Monk, I. 2006. British Radicalism and the Anti-Jacobins. In *The Cambridge History of Eighteenth-Century Political Thought*, ed. M. Goldie and R. Wokler, 660–687. Cambridge: Cambridge University Press.

Herzog, L. 2013a. *Inventing the Market. Smith, Hegel and Political Theory.* Oxford: Oxford University Press.

Herzog, L. 2013b. The Community of Commerce: Smith's Rhetoric of Sympathy in the Opening of the *Wealth of Nations*. *Philosophy and Rhetoric* 46 (1): 65–87.

Hill, J.E. 2016. *Adam Smith's Equality and the Pursuit of Happiness.* London and New York: Palgrave Macmillan.

Hill, L. 2006. Adam Smith and the Theme of Corruption. *Review of Politics* 68 (4): 636–662.

Hill, L. 2016. Adam Smith and Political Theory. In *Adam Smith: His Life, Thought, and Legacy*, ed. R.P. Hanley, 321–339. Princeton, NJ and Oxford: Princeton University Press.

Hill, L. 2020. *Adam Smith's Pragmatic Liberalism. The Science of Welfare*. London and New York: Palgrave Macmillan.

Hill, M., and W. Montag. 2015. *The Other Adam Smith.* Stanford: Stanford University Press.

Hirschman, A.O. 1977. *The Passions and the Interests. Political Arguments for Capitalism Before Its Triumph.* Princeton, NJ: Princeton University Press.

Hodgskin, T. 1825. *Labour Defended Against the Claims of Capital.* London: Knight and Lacey; Edinburgh: Baynes; Glasgow: M'Phun; Dublin: Westley and Tyrrel.

Höffner, J. 1941. *Wirtschaftsethik und Monopole in fünfzehnten und sechzehnten Jahrundert.* Jena: Verlag Gustav Fischer.

Hollander, S. 1973. *The Economics of Adam Smith.* London: Heinemann Educational Books; Toronto: University of Toronto Press.

Hume, D. 1752. *Political Discourses.* Edinburgh: Fleming.

Hutcheson, F. 1747. *A Short Introduction to Moral Philosophy in Three Books, Containing the Elements of Ethicks and the Law of Nature.* Glasgow: Foulis.

Hutcheson, F. 1755. *A System of Moral Philosophy in Three Books*, 2 vols. London: Foulis.

Hutchison, T.W. 1978. *On Revolutions and Progress in Economic Knowledge.* Cambridge: Cambridge University Press.

Ingham, G. 2008. *Capitalism.* Cambridge: Polity.

Jousse, J. 1771. *Traité de la justice criminelle de France*, 4 vols. Paris: Debure.

Jonsen, A.R., and S. Toulmin. 1988. *The Abuse of Casuistry. A History of Moral Reasoning.* Berkeley, Los Angeles, and London: University of California Press.

Kaplan, S.L. 1982. *The Famine Plot Persuasion in Eighteenth-Century France.* Philadelphia: The American Philosophical Society.

Kaplan, S.L. 1984. *Provisioning Paris. Merchants and Millers in the Grain and Flour Trade During the Eighteenth Century.* Cornell: Cornell University Press.

Kaplan, S.L. 2017. *Raisonner sur les blés. Essais sur les lumières économique.* Paris: Fayard.

Kennedy, G. 2008. *Adam Smith. A Moral Philosopher and His Political Economy.* London and New York: Routledge.

Langholm, O. 1998. *Legacy of Scholasticism in Economic Thought. Antecedents of Choice and Power.* Cambridge: Cambridge University Press.

Langholm O. 2006. Monopoly and Market Irregularities in Medieval Economic Thought: Traditions and Texts to A.D. 1500. *Journal of the History of Economic Thought* 28 (4): 395–411.

Larrere, C. 1992. *L'invention de l'économie au XVIIIe siècle. Du droit naturel à la physiocratie.* Paris: PUF.

Le Mercier de la Rivière, P.-P. 1767. *L'ordre naturel et essentiel des sociétés politiques.* London: Nourse.

Lessio, L. 1606. *De iustitia et iure.* Parisijs: Thierry.

Levy, D.M., and S. Peart. 2009. Adam Smith and the Place of Faction. In *Elgar Companion to Adam Smith*, ed. J.T. Joung, 335–345. Cheltenham: Edward Elgar.

Lopez, L. 1589. *Instructorium negotiantium duobus contentum libris.* Salmanticae: Bonardus.

Lopez, L. 1593. *Tractatus de contractibus et negotiationis duobus contenti libri*, 2 vols. Lugduni: Iuntarum.

Lubasz, H. 1995. Adam Smith and the 'Free Market'. In *Adam Smith's Wealth of Nations. New Interdisciplinary Essays*, ed. S. Copley and K. Sutherland. Manchester: Manchester University Press.

Lugo (de), I. 1652. *Disputationum de iustitia et iure*, 2 vols. Lugduni: Borde, Arnaud & Rigaud.

Magnusson, L. 2004. *The Tradition of Free Trade.* London and New York: Routledge.

Maifreda, G. 2012. *From Oikonomia to Political Economy. Constructing Economic Knowledge from the Renaissance to the Scientific Revolution.* Farnham and Burlington: Ashgate.

Malcomson, R.W. 1984. Workers Combinations in Eighteenth-Century England. In *The Origins of Anglo-American Radicalism*, ed. M. Jacob and J. Jacob, 149–161. London, Boston, and Sydney: Allen & Unwin.

Malynes, G. 1629. *Consuetudo, vel Lex Mercatoria.* London: Islip.

Marquardi, J. 1662. *Tractatus politico-iuridicus de iure mercatorum et commerciorum singulari*, 2 vols. Francofurti: Götz.
Martin, C. 2011. Adam Smith and Liberal Economics: Reading the Minimum Wage Debate of 1795–96. *Econ Journal Watch* 8 (2): 110–125.
Martin, C. 2015. Equity, Besides: Adam Smith and the Utility of Poverty. *Journal of the History of Economic Thought* 4: 559–581.
Mayers, M.L. 1983. *The Soul of Modern Economic Man. Ideas of Self-Interest, Thomas Hobbes to Adam Smith*. Chicago and London: University of Chicago Press.
McCulloch, J.R. 1824. Combination Laws—Restraints on Emigration, etc. *Edinburgh Review* XXXIX: 315–345.
McLean, I. 2006. *Adam Smith, Radical and Egalitarian. An Interpretation for the Twenty-First Century*. Edinburgh: Edinburgh University Press.
McNulty, P.J. 1973. Adam Smith's Concept of Labor. *Journal of the History of Ideas* 34 (3): 345–366.
Mercado (de), T. 1587 [1571]. *Suma de tratos y contratos*. Sevilla: Diaz.
Milgate, M., and S.C. Stimson. 2009. *After Adam Smith: A Century of Transformation in Politics and Political Economy*. Princeton, NJ and Oxford: Princeton University Press.
Millar, J. 1960 [1803]. The Advancement of Manufactures, Commerce, and the Arts, Since the Reign of William III; and the Tendency of This Advancement to Diffuse a Spirit of Liberty and Independence. In *John Millar of Glasgow, 1735–1801. His Life and Thought and His Contribution to Sociological Analysis*, ed. W.C. Lehmann, 326–333. Cambridge: Cambridge University Press.
Mingardi, A. 2018. Thomas Hodgskin, Rational Optimist. *Economic Affairs* 38 (1): 38–57.
Mizuta, H. 1967. *Adam Smith's Library. A Supplement to Bonar's Catalogue with a Checklist of the Whole Library*. Cambridge: Cambridge University Press.
Moher, J. 1988. From Suppression to Containment: Roots of Trade Union Law to 1825. In *British Trade Unionism, 1750–1850. The Formative Years*, ed. J. Rule, 74–97. London and New York: Longman.
Molina, L. 1601. *Disputationes de contractibus*. Venetiis: Collosino & Baretio.
Moore, J., and M. Silverthorne. 2002. Foreword. In *Natural Rights on the Threshold of the Scottish Enlightenment. The Writings of Gershom Carmichael*, ed. J. Moore and M. Silverthorne. Indianapolis: Liberty Fund.
More, T. 2002 [1516]. *Utopia*, ed. G.M. Logan and R.M. Adams. Cambridge: Cambridge University Press.

Morris, R.B. 1937. Criminal Conspiracy and Early Labor Combinations in New York. *Political Science Quarterly* 52 (1): 51–85.

Necker, J. 1820a [1775]. *Sur la législation et le commerce de grains*. In *Œuvres complètes de Mr. Necker, publiées par le baron de Staël*, 15 vols., Tome I. Paris: Treuttel et Würtz.

Necker, J. 1820b [1784]. *De l'administration des finances de la France*. In *Œuvres complètes de Mr. Necker, publiées par le baron de Staël*, 15 vols., Tome V. Paris: Treuttel et Würtz.

Nockleby, J.T. 1994. Two Theories of Competition in the Early 19th Century Labor Cases. *The American Journal of Legal History* 38 (4): 452–481.

Noell, E.S. 1995. Adam Smith on Economic Justice in the Labor Market. *Journal of the History of Economic Thought* 17 (2): 228–246.

O'Brien, D.P. 1970. *J.M. McCulloch. A Study in Classical Economics*. London: Allen & Unwin.

Ode, J. 1743. *Disputatio juridica inauguralis de monopoliis*. Traiecti ad Rhenum: van Megen.

Oñate (de), P. 1654. *De contractibus onerosis, tomus tertius*, 2 vols. Romae: Bernabò.

Ó Gráda, C. 2009. *Famine. A Short History*. Princeton, NJ and Oxford: Princeton University Press.

Ogose, T. 2003. Morality, Polity and Economy in Francis Hutcheson. In *The Rise of Political Economy in the Scottish Enlightenment*, ed. T. Sakamoto and H. Tanaka, 39–54. London and New York: Routledge.

Orth, J.V. 1987. English Combination Acts of the Eighteenth Century. *Law and History Review* 5 (1): 175–211.

Orth, J.V. 1991. *Combination and Conspiracy. A Legal History of Trade Unionism, 1721–1906*. Oxford: Clarendon Press.

Pack, S.P. 1991. *Capitalism as a Moral System. Adam Smith's Critique of the Free Market Economy*. Cheltenham and Northampton, MA: Edward Elgar.

Pasqualigo, Z. 1641. *Decisiones morales*. Verona: Merlum.

Perelman, M. 2000. *The Invention of Capitalism. Classical Political Economy and the Secret History of Primitive Accumulation*. Durham and London: Duke University Press.

Peri, G.D. 1673 [1651]. *I Frutti d'Albaro, overo Il Negotiante, parte terza*. Venetia: Hertz.

Perrot, J.-C. 1992. *Une histoire intellectuelle de l'économie politique, XVIIe-XVIIIe siécle*. Paris: EHESS.

Phelps Brown, E.H. 1976. The Labour Market. In *The Market and the State. Essays in Honour of Adam Smith*, ed. T. Wilson and A.S. Skinner, 243–259. Oxford: Clarendon Press.

Phillipson, N. 2010. *Adam Smith. An Enlightened Life*. New Haven, CT: Yale University Press.

Pignatelli, J. 1717 [1668–1697]. *Consultationes canonicae*, 11 vols. Lugduni: De Tournes.

Piotrowski, R. 1933. *Cartels and Trusts. Their Origin and Historical Development from the Economic and Legal Aspects*. London: Allen & Unwin.

Pocock, J.G.A. 1985. Josiah Tucker on Burke, Locke, and Price. A Study in Varieties of Eighteenth-Century Conservatism. In J.G.A. Pocock, *Virtue, Commerce, and History. Essays on Political Thought and History, Chiefly in Eighteenth Century*, 157–191. Cambridge and New York: Cambridge University Press.

Polanyi, K. 1944. *The Great Transformation. The Political and Economic Origins of Our Time*. New York and Toronto: Rinehart & Company.

Prodi, P. 2009. *Settimo non rubare. Furto e mercato nella storia dell'Occidente*. Bologna: il Mulino.

Pufendorf, S. 1729 [1672]. *Of the Law of Nature and Nations, Eight Books*. London: Walthoe, Wilkin, Bonwicke, Birt, Ward, Osborne.

Rasmussen, D.C. 2008. *The Problems and Promise of Commercial Society. Adam Smith's Response to Rousseau*. University Park, PA: The Pennsylvania State University Press.

Rasmussen, D.C. 2014. *The Pragmatic Enlightenment. Recovering the Liberalism of Hume, Smith, Montesquieu, and Voltaire*. Cambridge and New York: Cambridge University Press.

Rebello, F. 1608. *Opus de obligationibus iustitiae, religionis et caritatis*. Lugduni: Cardon.

Rebuffi, P. 1668 [1550]. *In constitutiones regias commentarius*. Amstelodami: Schipper.

Reginaldo, V. 1616. *Praxis fori poenitentialis ad direct confessarii*, 3 vols. Lugduni: Cardon.

Reyger (de), A. 1667 [1604]. *Thesaurus juris locupletissimus*, 2 vols. Francofurti and Lipsiae: Felgibeli.

Ricardo, D. 2004 [1951–1973]. *Letters, 1819–June 1821*. In *The Works and Correspondence of David Ricardo*, 11 vols., vol. 8, ed. P. Sraffa, with the collaboration of M.H. Dobb. Indianapolis: Liberty Fund.

Ron, A. 2008. Modern Natural Law Meets the Market: The Case of Adam Smith. *European Journal of Political Economy* 7 (2): 117–136.

Rosanvallon, P. 1999 [1979]. *Le capitalisme utopique. Histoire de l'idée de marché.* Paris: Seuil.

Rosolino, R. 2013. Vices tyranniques. Résistance au monopole, idéologie et marché à l'aube de la modernité. *Annales HSS* 68 (3): 793–819.

Rosolino, R. 2018. Resisting Economic Conspiracies: Adam Smith, the (Labour) Market, and the Moral Basis of Antimonopolistic Resistance. *History of Political Thought* 39 (2): 297–324.

Rothschild, E. 2001. *Economic Sentiments. Adam Smith, Condorcet and the Enlightenment.* London and Cambridge, MA: Harvard University Press.

Rothschild, E., and A. Sen. 2006. Adam Smith's Economics. In *The Cambridge Companion to Adam Smith*, ed. K. Haakonssen, 319–365. Cambridge and New York: Cambridge University Press.

Rubin, I.I. 1979 [1929]. *A History of Economic Thought.* London: Ink Links.

Sabelli, M.A. 1733 [1685]. *Summa diversorum tractatuum*, 8 vols. Parmae: Monti.

Salas (de), I. 1617. *Commentarii in sucundam secundae D. Thome de Contractibus.* Lugduni: Cardon.

Salon, M.B. 1608. *Controversiae de iustitia et iure, atque de contractibus & commercijs humanis, licitis ac illicitis*, 2 vols. Venetiis: Baretio.

Sampson, M. 1988. Laxity and Liberty in Seventeenth-Century English Political Thought. In *Conscience and Casuistry in Early Modern Europe*, ed. E. Leites, 72–118. Cambridge and Paris: Cambridge UP/Editions MSH.

Sandmo, A. 2016. Adam Smith and Modern Economics. In *Adam Smith: His Life, Thought, and Legacy*, ed. R.P. Hanley, 231–246. Princeton, NJ and Oxford: Princeton University Press.

Savary, J. 1675. *Le parfait negociant ou instruction generale pour ce qui regarde le commerce.* Paris: Guignard.

Savelli, R. 1987. Between Law and Morals: Interest in the Dispute on Exchanges During the 16th Century. In *The Courts and the Development of Commercial Law*, ed. V. Piergiovanni, 39–102. Berlin: Duncker & Humblot.

Scaccia, S. 1619. *Tractatus de commerciis et cambio.* Romae: Brugiotti.

Schlisser, E. 2017. *Adam Smith. Systematic Philosopher and Public Thinker.* Oxford and New York: Oxford University Press.

Schmidtz, D. 2016. Adam Smith on Freedom. In *Adam Smith. His Life, Thought, and Legacy*, ed. R.P. Hanley, 208–227. Princeton, NJ and Oxford: Princeton University Press.

Schmitt, C. 1976 [1932]. *The Concept of the Political.* New Brunswick: Rutgers University Press.

Schumpeter, J.A. 2006 [1954]. *History of Economic Analysis.* London and New York: Routledge.

Schuster, G.F. 1686. *Dissertatio juridica in Pragmaticam Imp. Rom. German. Sanctionem, de monopoliis.* Gissae Hassorum: Mulleri.

Schwartz, D. 2019. Just Persuasion in Baroque Electoral Ethics. *Ephemerides Theologicae Lovanienses* 95 (4): 595–614.

Sen, A. 2011. Uses and Abuses of Adam Smith. *History of Political Economy* 43 (2): 257–271.

Sheehan, J., and D. Wahrman. 2015. *Invisible Hands. Self-Organization and the Eighteenth-Century.* Chicago and London: University of Chicago Press.

Shelton, G. 1981. *Dean Tucker and Eighteenth-Century Economic and Political Thought.* London: Macmillan.

Smith, A. 1805 [1776]. *An Inquiry into the Nature and Causes of the Wealth of Nations* (The Eleventh Edition; with Notes, Supplementary Chapters, and a Life of Dr. Smith, by William Playfair), 3 vols. London: Cadell and Davies.

Smith, A. 1976 [1776]. *An Inquiry into the Nature and Causes of the Wealth of Nations*, 2 vols., ed. R.H. Campbell and A.S. Skinner. Oxford: Oxford University Press.

Smith, A. 1978. *Lectures on Jurisprudence*, ed. R.L. Meek, D.D. Raphael, and P.G. Stein. Oxford: Oxford University Press.

Soto (de), D. 1582 [1553]. *De iustitia et iure.* Lugduni: Honorato.

Stack, D. 1998. *Nature and Artifice. The Life and Thought of Thomas Hodgskin (1787–1869).* Woodbridge: Boydell.

Stanziani, A. 2007. Spéculation. In *Dictionnaire historique de l'économie-droit, XVIIIe-XX siècles*, sous la direction de A. Stanziani. Paris: Maison des Sciences de l'Homme/Réseau Euroéen Droit et Société.

Stein, P. 1979. Adam Smith's Jurisprudence—Between Morality and Economics. *Cornell Law Review* 64 (4): 621–638.

Steiner, P. 2006. Le débat sur la liberté du commerce des grains (1750–1775). In *Histoire du libéralisme en Europe*, sous la direction de P. Nemo and J. Petitot, 255–278. Paris: PUF.

Steuart, J. 1767. *An Inquiry into the Principles of Political Economy*, 2 vols. London: Millar & Cadell.

Stewart, D. 1980 [1794]. *Account of the Life and Writings of Adam Smith*, LL.D. In A. Smith, *Essays on Philosophical Subjects*, ed. W.P.D. Wightman and J.C. Bryce, 269–332. Oxford: Oxford University Press.

Stirati, A. 1994. *The Theory of Wages in Classical Economics. A Study of Adam Smith, David Ricardo and Their Contemporaries.* Aldershot and Brookfield: Edward Elgar.

Suarez, F. 1742 [1608–1609]. *Opus de virtute et statu religionis*, 4 vols. In F. Suarez, *Opera omnia hactenus edita* [1740–1751], 23 vols. Venetiis: ex typographia Balleoniana.

Taylor, W.L. 1965. *Francis Hutcheson and David Hume as Predecessors of Adam Smith*. Durham: Duke University Press.

Teichgraeber, III, R.F. 1986. *'Free Trade' and Moral Philosophy. Rethinking the Sources of Adam Smith's Wealth of Nations*. Durham: Duke University Press.

Tepati, A. 1682. *Compendium decisionum et variarum sententiarum juri canonici civilis et criminalis*, 3 vols. Vratislaviae Silesiorum: Fellgibeli.

Thelwall, J. 1796. *The Rights of Nature, Against the Usurpations of Establishments*, Letter I. London: Symonds and March.

Thompson, E.P. 1991 [1963]. *The Making of the English Working Class*. London: Penguin.

Thompson, N.W. 1984. *The People's Science. The Popular Political Economy of Exploitation and Crisis 1816–34*. Cambridge: Cambridge University Press.

Thompson, N. 1998. *The Real Rights of Man. Political Economies for the Working Class 1775–1850*. London and Sterling, VA: Pluto Press.

Tierney, B. 1997. *The Idea of Natural Rights. Studies on Natural Rights, Natural Law, and Church Law 1150–1625*. Atlanta: Scholars Press.

Tooze, A. 2018. *Crashed. How a Decade of Financial Crises Changed the World*. New York: Viking.

Trevelyan, G.M. 1922. *British History in the Nineteenth Century and After (1782–1919)*. London, New York, and Toronto: Longmans.

Tucker, J. 1750. *A Brief Essay on the Advantages and Disadvantages Which Respectively Attend France and Great Britain with Regard to Trade*. London: Trye.

Tucker, J. 1931 [1755]. *The Elements of Commerce and Theory of Taxes* (*A Preliminary Discourse, Setting Forth the natural Disposition, or instinctive Inclination of Mankind Towards Commerce*). In J. Tucker, *A Selection from His Economic and Political Writings*, 55–219. New York: Columbia University Press.

Turchetti, M. 1999. 'Il faut obéir à Dieu plutôt qu'aux hommes': Aux sources théologiques du droit de résistance au siècle de la Réforme. In *Le droit de résistance, XIIe–XXe siècle*, Textes réunis par J.-C. Zancarini, 71–103. Lyon: École Normale Supérieure.

Turgot, A.R.J. 2011a [1766]. *Reflections on the Formation and Distribution of Wealth*. In *The Turgot Collection. Writings, Speeches, and Letters of Anne Robert Jacques Turgot, Baron de Laune*, ed. D. Gordon, 5–65. Auburn: Mises Institute.

Turgot, A.R.J. 2011b [1759]. *In Praise of Gournay.* In *The Turgot Collection. Writings, Speeches, and Letters of Anne Robert Jacques Turgot, Baron de Laune*, ed. D. Gordon, 100–127. Auburn: Mises Institute.

Turpin, P. 2011. *The Moral Rhetoric of Political Economy. Justice and Modern Economic Thought.* London and New York: Routledge.

Verani, C.F. 1703–1708. *Juris canonici universi commentarius paratitlaris*, 5 vols. Monachii: Jaecklini.

Villalobos (de), H. 1636. *Summa de la Theologia Moral y Canonica*, 2 vols. Barcelona: de Cormellas.

Viner, J. 1927. Adam Smith and Laissez-Faire. *Journal of Political Economy* 35 (2): 198–232.

Wallas, G. 1898. *The Life of Francis Place, 1771–1854.* London, New York, and Bombay: Longmans.

Webb, S., and B. Webb. 1911 [1898]. *The History of Trade Unionism.* London: Longman.

Weber, M. 1978 [1922]. *Economy and Society*, ed. G. Roth and C. Wittich. Berkeley, Los Angeles, and London: University of California Press.

Werhane, P.H. 1991. *Adam Smith and His Legacy for Modern Capitalism.* Oxford: Oxford University Press.

Weststeijn, A. 2012. *Commercial Republicanism in the Dutch Golden Age. The Political Thought of Johan & Pieter de la Court.* Leiden and Boston: Brill.

Willis, K. 1979. The Role in Parliament of the Economic Ideas of Adam Smith, 1776–1800. *History of Political Economy* 11 (4): 505–544.

Winch, D. 1978. *Adam Smith's Politics. An Essay on Historiographic Revision.* Cambridge: Cambridge University Press.

Winch, D. 1996. *Riches and Poverty. An Intellectual History of Political Economy in Britain, 1750–1834.* Cambridge: Cambridge University Press.

Young, B.W. 1996. Christianity, Commerce and the Canon: Josiah Tucker and Richard Woodward on Political Economy. *History of European Ideas* 22: 384–400.

Young, J.T. 2005. Unintended Order and Intervention: Adam Smith's Theory of the Role of the State. *History of Political Economy* 37: 91–119.

Young, J.T. 2008. Law and Economics in the Protestant Natural Tradition: Samuel Pufendorf, Francis Hutcheson, and Adam Smith. *Journal of the History of Economic Thought* 30 (3): 283–296.

Index

R. Rosolino, *Countervailing Powers*,
https://doi.org/10.1007/978-3-030-37802-8

The manufacturer's authorised representative in the EU is Springer Nature Customer Service Centre GmbH, Europaplatz 3, 69115 Heidelberg, Germany. If you have any concerns regarding our products, please contact ProductSafety@springernature.com

Printed and bound by CPI Group (UK) Ltd, Croydon, CR0 4YY
22/09/2026
02221054-0018